Nourishing Your Whole Self

Nourishing Your Whole Self

A Cookbook with Feelings

Marci Izard

PELICAN PUBLISHING COMPANY
Gretna 2015

*The word "Pelican" and the depiction of a pelican are
trademarks of Pelican Publishing Company, Inc., and are
registered in the U.S. Patent and Trademark Office.*

Library of Congress Cataloging-in-Publication Data

Izard, Marci.
  Nourishing your whole self : a cookbook with feelings / by Marci Izard.
      pages cm
  Includes index.
    ISBN 978-1-4556-2079-1 (hardcover : alk. paper) — ISBN 978-1-4556-
2080-7 (e-book) 1. Cooking. 2. Dinners and dining—Psychological
aspects. I. Title.
  TX714.I935 2015
  641.5'4—dc23
                                                    2015007923

Printed in China
Published by Pelican Publishing Company, Inc.
1000 Burmaster Street, Gretna, Louisiana 70053

Faith made this book. I dedicate it to the love that surrounds me, and especially to my mom, dad, and sister, Blair.

contents

preface

As I sit here sipping red wine and snacking on kalamata olives, Havarti with dill, and hunks of creamily delicious organic goat cheese, I am reflecting on the undeniable reality that I do not have a perfect diet, or all the answers on eating right. Well into my adult years, I no longer wrestle with an eating disorder, but I do still engage in occasional "disorderly eating"—such as turning to food when I'm excited . . . bored . . . anxious . . . and, apparently, have writer's block. I am obviously a work in progress. The point is that I'm working. And that is what this book is about.

It's *not* about dieting or cutting calories, carbohydrates, caffeine, or cabernet. It *is* about learning about yourself, compassionately reconnecting with your feelings, and allowing raised awareness to naturally shift you toward greater balance overall. You can achieve this balance through delicious recipes, and the implications are universal.

In the coming pages, I will explain the concept more and share some of my all-time favorite dishes. I hope this book speaks to you and delights your senses. It has been a labor of love.

In my heart, I believe that as we tune in and become more conscious individuals, we raise our own capacities for living well and simultaneously uplift everyone else's too. To me, that is inspiring—and *delicious*. So let's dig in . . . and dig deep!

introduction

I want to help you connect with the internal wisdom that is reflected in your flesh. This book is about tuning in to your body and the way you feel, in order to become more present and self-aware. Then you can make conscious choices that align with your intuition. It is a path to nourishing your whole self.

There are infinite ways to cultivate internal connection, but here, the focus is on doing it with food. I have found that bringing feeling and connection into mealtime creates a healthy shift: as I have become more conscious of how foods make me feel, I've naturally tended to eat better. At the same time, that willingness to go within and raise my self-awareness has fine-tuned my life in many other ways too.

Allow me to explain.

If you have flipped through this cookbook, you have probably noticed that it is pretty unique. Instead of "Appetizers," "Main Dishes," "Desserts," etc., the chapters here are: "Refreshed," "Peaceful," "Comforted," "Treated," and "Indulged." These categories are loosely based on everything from nutritional content and cooking methods to Ayurveda, Taoist dietary principles, and my own emotional responses. In other words, they are rooted in research and yet entirely subjective at the same time.

Eating food is ideally a positive experience, and each category in this book is particularly optimistic. The only catch is that dishes that lean toward "indulged" should be enjoyed in moderation. One Double-Chocolate Brownie can lift you up and make you feel elated. Eating the whole pan can weigh you down and make you feel depressed. Trust me, I know.

But the ultimate purpose of the categories is deeper than picking foods based on your mood or taking my word on their effects. In the end, everything in this book goes back to the theme of internal connection. The quotes and photographs are meant to inspire you to tune in. The recipe categories are reminders of the correlation between what we eat and how we feel, encouraging you to connect to how *you* feel.

Here's a story about why this has worked for me. I'll preface this by saying that I'm tempted not to share it. Part of me would like to have you believe that I've got it all figured out. But since I'm trying to get more comfortable with the distressing reality that I can't have everyone's approval, and I essentially render myself ineffective if I even seek that, I'll go ahead and give you the straight poop (sorry for using that term in a cookbook).

It was sophomore year of college. . . . After a pretty rowdy night out that admittedly involved a fair amount of underage drinking, I got in around two o'clock and decided to do what makes most sense for that time of night: order food. For whatever reason, no one else was up for a late-night chow down on this particular Friday, so instead of calling in something heavy and greasy like a pepperoni pizza (this story makes my stomach hurt), I got wings—honey barbeque. But then, one of my friends nonchalantly said something about "sharing" my order. A chill went down my spine.

Long story short, the wings guy called from downstairs. I retrieved the order and proceeded to hoard it. I hunkered down in a stairwell nook and frantically demolished the whole tray before anyone could see me and bum a bite. When I finally went back upstairs empty-handed to a concerned group, I relayed some BS story about meeting a girl in the dorm lobby and sharing my wings with her. I wish I could blame it on the alcohol. I finally fessed up a few years later.

I share this because it is my truth. I don't always eat healthy or feel immune to occasional bouts of shame. I write and talk about conscious eating as a means for empowered living perhaps because, as they say, you teach what you most need to learn. I have had varying degrees of eating disorders over the years, and in many ways this continues to be a work in progress. And I know it's not just me.

We live in a world that's equally obsessed with food and being thin, and in that environment, a peaceful perspective is not only hard, it's also unnatural, unless you look within. Here's how you can.

1. *Feel.*

Remember my categories? Forget them. They were a tool to get you here—to raise awareness of the profoundly underappreciated connection between what we eat and how we feel. Once that's acknowledged, it's time to move beyond words and labels. Now, we feel.

That can begin, quite simply, with breathing. When you take deep, conscious breaths, your nervous system switches gears. After just one minute of slow, focused breathing, your senses awaken, salivary glands activate, endorphins rev up, digestion kicks in, and brain capacity expands. Present, deliberate breath is the first step to feeling. So when it's time to eat, breathe! When you first sit down, take a few conscious breaths.

From there, mindful eating—or, as I like to think of it, "grateful eating"— can also help you to be present and connected. Notice colors, textures, and aromas. Put your fork down between bites. Chew slowly and savor. Creating a beautiful setting helps me. Many times that means lighting a candle and turning on my 365-days-a-year Christmas lights. Soft music is good too. Try to skip the TV.

Then at least once during a meal, take another conscious breath and feel your body. In other words, without mentally judging anything, notice the sensations under your skin. Feel your feet planted on the floor . . . the tingling in your hands . . . the tension in your head. Doing this helps you relax and brings you into the present moment—which is where genuine connection lies.

Bear in mind that none of this means that in order to eat a meal, you need to sit alone on the floor in a cross-legged position with your eyes closed, channeling a monk. I do this in moments. I'd be lying if I said I do it all the time . . . but when I do remember, I don't only eat better, I enjoy my food more too. The meditation below can help build your feeling muscle to make this brand of connection a more natural way of eating—and living.

I practice some form of meditation in the morning and evening, even if just for five or ten minutes, and I bring moments of it into mealtime. As you give it a try, remember that (contrary to what a lot of people think) meditation does not require that you stop thinking. Thinking is what the mind does! So rather than telling your brain to shut up, practice simply noticing your thoughts instead. Be the observer—see your thoughts, and without attaching to them or getting drawn into their spiral, let each thought pass. Over and over again, gently come back to the moment and the physical experience of your body.

Get into a comfortable seated position. If you are resting on the floor, consider using a pillow to elevate your hips.

Feel the ground beneath you, and permit gravity's support. Allow it to pull tension out of your body and deep into the earth.

Notice the voice that is speaking in your head—the inaudible, ever-present voice. Take a moment to notice what it says. Watch its story like a movie. Without getting involved, simply observe. See your thoughts as they come up, and then let them gently pass.

Take a deep, nourishing breath and relax your head. Un-crinkle your scalp. Soften the muscles in your face. Feel.

Carry that sense of ease down your neck and into your shoulders.

Feel your letting go.

Notice your arms. From your biceps . . . into your elbows . . . forearms . . . and hands . . . feel the sensation. Take time to experience the vitality in your palms and the light pulsing in your fingertips.

Move attention to your heart. Take an expansive breath into the front and back of your chest.

Relax your belly.

Allow feeling and connection to glide down your spine and into your seat.

Feel your roots and energy flowing into your legs. . . .

Allow awareness to slowly move all the way down into your feet. Feel your toes and contact to the earth.

Breathe.

Witness your entire body.

Take note of thoughts. Notice how they could turn into emotions . . . but in this still and peaceful moment, you release them instead.

Continue to feel your body letting go, as you do the same with each thought. Simply breathe. Be still. Release.

2. Say grace.

For me, this is a prayer. For you it may be a conversation with your most empowered self. Either way, the point is to be actively grateful and explicitly open to receiving insight. I like to say thank you and ask for guidance, even if it's just as simple as saying: "Thank you for this food. Please help me to experience and appreciate every bite." I say grace before a meal (often just in my head) and whenever else I need to tune in and re-center, which is a lot.

3. Forgive yourself.

There is a lot of shame associated with eating. Sometimes we all (over) indulge or fall back into old habits. At least I do. And I know from experience that beating myself up over dietary indiscretions doesn't help. It impairs my connectedness instead. So rather than falling into a pit of despair, I now try to just let it go and trust that, with my ongoing noble efforts, rebalancing will naturally occur.

4. Be open.

Connection hinges on openness. Relating to food, that could mean sharing these ideas, sampling new recipes, and cooking for others. In the bigger picture, it may entail stepping out of your comfort zone and saying yes to new books, services, videos, people, places, classes—you name it. The key is being nonjudgmental. Judging yourself and others is not being open. I have found that simply desiring connection with your intuition starts to attract more wisdom to you, so it's imperative that you be open to receiving it in whatever capacity it comes. Then, insights and progress are more likely to last when they're shared.

This cookbook concept is not about dieting or losing weight. And it's only about looks to the extent that feeling good and living well ultimately facilitate appearing good too.

When you make it a priority to tune in, your eating habits may or may not change. That's secondary. The point is deeper and more comprehensive than what your plate contains, what the scale reads, or even the broad elements of mindful eating.

This is about becoming a more centered person. It's about the continuous practice of tuning in and *feeling* with grace, openness, and, ultimately, unconditional self-love. As I have worked on this, my way of being and my subsequent choices have come to reflect that sense of balance. These days, I crave fresh greens after eating junk food. Don't get me wrong. I still love my cookies, wine, cheese, all kinds of carbs, and occasionally a few good wings, but at the same time, when I practice what I preach, I naturally lean toward healthy moderation. I'm also calmer, more authentic, and more connected in other areas too—like within my spiritual path, my relationships, and my passions.

I hope some of this connects with you as well. Please chew these ideas over as you cook and enjoy the eclectic blend of recipes I have compiled.

It is my prayer that the experience will *nourish your whole self.*

Nourishing Your Whole Self

feel Refreshed

Feel clean and vibrant.

Experience energy, openness, and awareness.

These are the healthiest recipes in this cookbook. They are low in fat and calories and high in vitamins, minerals, and disease-fighting phytochemicals. These dishes contain mostly whole foods that are uncomplicated for the body to process and digest—foods that will not weigh you down but rather will promote lightness and wellbeing. Clean, nutrient-rich recipes can buoy your energy and increase your vitality and delight. Eat these foods to refresh your vibrancy, inside and out!

Tomato-Avocado-Kalamata Salad

Arugula gives this radiant salad a lively base. The dish is a vibrant blend of color, texture, and pungent flavor, with olives and avocado making it simultaneously grounding and enlivening.

Serves 4

1 cup arugula
4 leaves red-leaf lettuce
3 radishes, sliced
2 tomatoes, thickly sliced
2 avocados, peeled and sliced

20 pitted kalamata olives, sliced
4 tsp. extra-virgin olive oil, divided
1 tsp. balsamic vinegar, divided
Salt and freshly ground black pepper

Divide the arugula among 4 plates. Over the leaves, evenly distribute the red-leaf lettuce, radish slices, tomato, avocado, and olives. Drizzle 1 tsp. oil and ¼ tsp. vinegar over each serving. Add salt and freshly ground black pepper to taste.

"Awareness is the greatest agent for change." Eckhart Tolle

Tomato and Zucchini "Pasta" Salad

This sweetly fragrant seasonal salad is light and alluring. Fresh basil gives the dish a calming effect, while zucchini facilitates balance. The grape tomatoes bring it all to life.

Serves 4

2 small zucchinis
10 oz. grape tomatoes, sliced in half
¼ cup chopped fresh basil
2 gloves garlic, pressed

2 tbsp. balsamic vinegar
1 tbsp. extra-virgin olive oil
Salt to taste

Using a julienne peeler or mandoline, thinly slice the zucchini into strips that resemble spaghetti. You may need to use a knife to (carefully!) finish the job.

Add the zucchini strips to a large bowl with the remaining ingredients. Toss well.

"Forgiving means forgetting." *Many Wonderful Things*

Nutty Bean Salad

This cool, nutty salad is loaded with energetic potential. It has a subtle sweetness and hearty crunch that invigorates the senses, while the buttery beans add a cleansing lightness. Folk tradition links vitamin E, which is abundant in almonds, with healing a broken heart.

Serves 2

1 cup frozen lima beans or shelled
    edamame, defrosted
¼ cup unsalted almonds, roughly
    chopped
2 tbsp. raisins

2 tbsp. sunflower seeds
½ lemon
2 tbsp. extra-virgin olive oil
1 tbsp. balsamic vinegar
Salt and freshly ground black pepper

In a medium bowl, combine the beans, almonds, raisins, and sunflower seeds. Squeeze in all the juice from the lemon half. Toss with the oil, vinegar, and salt and freshly ground black pepper to taste.

"The whole is more than the sum of its parts." Aristotle

Side-Dish Salad

This beautiful, detoxifying side dish is bold and zesty. The lemon, red onion, and cilantro make it powerfully purifying and intrinsically awakening. It will rev up your energy and immunity.

Serves 2-4

1 avocado, peeled and chopped
¼ cup chopped red onion
2 tomatoes, chopped
2 tbsp. extra-virgin olive oil

Juice of ½ lemon
½ cup chopped cilantro
Salt and freshly ground black pepper

Mix all the ingredients in a medium bowl. Let the mixture stand for at least 20 minutes. Serve with chicken, fish, or maybe even chips!

"What if the body is actually a mirror of how we live our lives?"
Dr. Lissa Rankin

Watermelon, Cucumber, and Feta Salad

This radiant, highly hydrating salad is pretty and powerful! Watermelon and cucumber are over 90 percent water. This playful combination is captivatingly refreshing and salty-sweet.

Serves 6

¼ watermelon, peeled, seeded, and cut into chunks
2 cucumbers, cut into chunks
¼ cup chopped mint leaves (plus extra leaves for garnish)

1 lb. feta cheese, cut into chunks
2 tbsp. balsamic vinegar

On a large dish, spread out half of the cucumber. Add half of the watermelon on top. Repeat with the remaining cucumber and watermelon.

Sprinkle mint over the mixture, and then scatter hunks of feta cheese throughout.

Drizzle vinegar over the top.

"Every time you smile at someone, it is an action of love, a gift to that person, a beautiful thing." Mother Teresa

Classic Greek Salad

This Mediterranean delight is a treat disguised as salad. It is best to use local tomatoes, a seasonal cucumber, and the highest-quality feta you can find. The cheese and olives make this simple recipe rich, while the raw veggies freshen it up. It's a bold, vibrant, and joyful mix—Greek, through and through.

Serves 6

4 tomatoes, cut into wedges
1 cucumber, sliced
½ medium red onion, sliced
1 tbsp. dried oregano leaves
3 tbsp. extra-virgin olive oil

Salt
10-20 pitted kalamata olives
4-6 oz. Greek feta cheese, sliced
Freshly ground black pepper

Place the tomatoes, cucumber, red onion, oregano, oil, and salt to taste in a large bowl. Gently toss to coat. Transfer the salad to a large dish or a clean bowl and scatter the olives and feta throughout. Top with freshly ground black pepper to taste.

"You are never too old to set another goal or to dream a new dream." C. S. Lewis

Sesame-Kale Salad

Ancient color therapy links green foods with renewal. Kale's rejuvenating effects are amplified in this salad thanks to the cleansing properties of garlic and ginger. And it's delicious too.

Serves 2

¾ tsp. minced fresh ginger
I tsp. minced fresh garlic
I ½ tsp. rice vinegar
I ½ tsp. soy sauce
I ½ tsp. honey

I tbsp. toasted sesame oil
I tbsp. extra-virgin olive oil
I small-medium bunch kale
¾ tsp. white sesame seeds

In a small bowl, combine the ginger, garlic, vinegar, soy sauce, honey, and oils. Stir well.

Remove bulky stems from the kale and discard. Tear the leaves into pieces. Pour the ginger mixture over the kale in a large bowl, and use your hands to massage the leaves for about 3 minutes, until they turn bright green and significantly reduce in volume. Top each serving with a sprinkle of sesame seeds.

"I'm wholehearted about whatever I do." Melinda Gates

Peanut Buttery Greens

This sweet and salty salad is ready in a jiff! It's an interesting mix that's nutritious and uplifting. For best results, use a combination of greens such as baby kale, spinach, chard, or another lettuce of your choice.

Serves 4

4 tsp. extra-virgin olive oil
2 tsp. all-natural peanut butter
1 tsp. soy sauce

1 tsp. honey
4 cups loosely packed mesclun greens

Mix the oil, peanut butter, soy sauce, and honey in a small bowl. Pour the mixture over the greens in a larger bowl and toss well to coat.

"Within you resides the very same spark of infinite energy and limitless potential that animates all living things." Panache Desai

Creamy Cucumber Salad

This cool salad combines the cleansing properties of cucumber, vinegar, and garlic with the probiotics in plain yogurt. The mixture gets healthy digestive juices flowing, to leave you feeling fresh.

Serves 2

1 cucumber, cut into chunks
¼ cup low-fat plain yogurt (not Greek)
Salt to taste
1 clove garlic, pressed

1 tsp. dried dill
½ tsp. white vinegar
1-2 tbsp. crumbled feta cheese
  (optional)

Combine all the ingredients in a medium bowl, and toss well to coat.

"Anytime the mind says, 'It's too much,' question it."
Byron Katie

Creamy Avocado Dressing

Avocado's natural fat and creamy consistency give this dressing a hint of indulgence, but the lemon and garlic make it sparkle. This combination is both tasty and nutritious.

Makes 1 cup

1 avocado, peeled and pitted	¼ tsp. salt
2 tbsp. extra-virgin olive oil	2 cloves garlic, peeled
2 tbsp. lemon juice	9 tbsp. water

Combine all the ingredients in a small food processor. Blend until smooth and creamy. Toss the dressing with any salad.

Salad options:

1. Combine black beans and chopped cilantro, tomato, green onion, lettuce, red bell pepper, cucumber, and radish.

2. For a heartier dish, prepare a cobb salad with the following ingredients all chopped up: 1 cup lettuce, 1 cup spinach, 1 yellow or red bell pepper, 1 cucumber, 2 tomatoes, 1 avocado, 1 cup cooked chicken, 1 cup feta cheese, 8 slices crisp bacon, 2 hardboiled eggs.

"A deep change for me was realizing I'd have to take the time to know what I *feel*, in order to know who I am and who I want to be." Maria Shriver

Tabbouleh

Fiber-rich bulgur wheat, pungent parsley, and awakening lemon juice make this Middle Eastern salad clean and clearing. Parsley promotes digestion and flushes out toxins, and the salad's tangy flavor effectively draws energy in. This is a wonderful warm-weather recipe.

Serves 6

½ cup uncooked bulgur wheat
½ cup boiling water
3-4 plum tomatoes, diced
2 green onions, finely chopped
1-2 bunches parsley (if it's a large bunch, just use 1), finely chopped

1 clove garlic, pressed
2 tbsp. mint leaves, finely chopped
Juice of 2 lemons
3 tbsp. extra-virgin olive oil
Salt and freshly ground black pepper

Place the bulgur in a medium bowl. Pour the boiling water on top, and allow the mixture to stand for about 1 hour, until the water is absorbed.

In the meantime, combine the tomatoes, green onions, parsley, garlic, mint, lemon juice, oil, and salt and freshly ground black pepper to taste in a separate bowl. Set aside.

When the bulgur is ready, stir it into the tomato mixture. Add salt and toss well. Ideally, let the salad stand for a few hours before serving.

"Everyone who seeks, finds." Matthew 7:8

Beet and Bulgur Salad

This unique salad draws energy in. Its lemon-curry dressing, vibrant colors, and coarse texture are sassily stimulating. This dish will make you feel as bright as it looks.

Serves 6–8

1 cup bulgur
1 cup boiling water
½ cup extra-virgin olive oil
3 tbsp. lemon juice
1 tbsp. curry powder
1 large clove garlic
1-inch piece ginger, peeled

1 tsp. salt
3-4 golden beets, scrubbed and finely chopped
3 green onions, chopped
4-6 radishes, finely chopped
1 cucumber, finely chopped

Place the bulgur in a medium bowl. Pour the boiling water on top, and allow the mixture to stand for about 1 hour, until the water is absorbed.

Place the oil, lemon juice, curry powder, garlic, and salt in a blender and pulse until thoroughly combined. Set aside.

Place the chopped veggies in a large bowl. When the bulgur is ready, add it in, and then pour half the dressing on top. Toss well to coat. Refrigerate remaining dressing.

"The best way out is always through." Robert Frost

Creamy Cauliflower Soup

This naturally creamy concoction combats inertia and gets your chi (life force) flowing. As cauliflower promotes mental and physical fluidity, this soup may make you feel more clear and open.

Serves 4

6-8 cloves garlic, separated but
    unpeeled, ends trimmed
2 tbsp. extra-virgin olive oil
I large shallot, thinly sliced
Salt

I head cauliflower, chopped into
    I-inch pieces
I tsp. dried thyme leaves
24 oz. vegetable broth
Freshly ground black pepper

Preheat oven to 350 degrees. Place the garlic on a sheet of aluminum foil. Roast for 20 minutes, until soft. Let the cloves cool (about 5-10 minutes), then peel and mash them in a small bowl.

In a large pot, heat the olive oil. Add the shallot and salt to taste, and cook for about 3 minutes. Add the garlic, cauliflower, thyme, and broth. Bring the mixture to a boil, reduce the heat, and simmer, covered, for 25 minutes.

Puree the soup using an immersion blender or standard blender in batches. Do not overprocess. Reheat the soup as necessary.

Add salt to taste. Top each serving with freshly ground black pepper to taste.

"Our life always expresses the result of our dominant thoughts."
Soren Kierkegaard

Tex-Mex Chicken Soup

This snazzy soup is joy in a bowl. Cilantro, avocado, tomato, and spoonfuls of other lively ingredients make it deliciously rejuvenating. Opt for a high-quality broth and consider making the soup a day in advance to allow the fabulous flavors to fully infuse.

Serves 10-12

12 cups chicken broth
4 cloves garlic, minced
1 onion, diced
½ cup chopped carrots
1 green, yellow, or red bell pepper, diced
1 cooked rotisserie chicken
1 (15.25 oz.) can corn, rinsed and drained

1½ cups chopped cilantro, divided
5 tomatoes, diced
2 limes
½ tsp. cumin
Salt
2-3 avocados, peeled and chopped
Shredded Jack cheese

In a large pot, bring the chicken broth to a light boil.

Add the garlic, onion, carrots, and pepper. Simmer for 10 minutes.

Add the meat from the chicken, corn, ½ cup cilantro, diced tomatoes, juice from 1 lime, cumin, and salt to taste. Continue to simmer for 20 minutes. Top each serving with extra cilantro, avocado, Jack cheese, and a slice of lime.

"Did you know that 80% of the information we receive comes through our eyes? And if you compare light energy to musical scales it would only be one octave the naked eye could see, which is right in the middle?" Louie Schwartzberg

Butternut-Leek Soup

This vibrant bowl of sunshine tastes as magnificent as it looks. It is simple and pure, with an all-natural, creamy consistency that's sure to boost your mood!

Serves 2

8 cloves garlic, separated but unpeeled
1 tbsp. extra-virgin olive oil
2 leeks, finely chopped
1 butternut squash, peeled, cored, and cut into chunks

2½ cups vegetable broth
½ tsp. salt
Freshly ground black pepper

Preheat oven to 350 degrees.

Slice off and discard the bottoms (stems) of the garlic cloves. Place the unpeeled cloves on a sheet of foil, and bake for 20 minutes, until soft. Afterward, let them cool for 5–10 minutes, then peel.

In a large pot, heat the oil over medium heat. Add the leeks and cook, stirring often, for about 5 minutes. Add the roasted garlic, squash, broth, and salt. Bring the mixture to a boil, then reduce the heat to a simmer and cover. Cook for 15–20 minutes. Carefully puree the soup with an immersion blender, or standard blender in batches. Reheat the soup as necessary.

Top with freshly ground black pepper to taste.

"Seeing how one phenomenon—yourself—exists, you can also know the nature of all other phenomena." Dalai Lama

Shrimp Ceviche

This high-protein, nutrient-dense appetizer is bursting with brightness and vitality. Its spicy tang will stimulate your senses without spoiling your appetite.

Serves 4

1 cup chopped cooked cocktail shrimp
   (about ⅓ lb.)
Juice of 1 lime
1 cup chopped tomato
1 avocado, chopped
¼ cup minced red onion

½ jalapeno, seeded and minced
½ cup chopped fresh cilantro
Salt and freshly ground black pepper
   to taste
Tortilla chips for serving

Combine all the ceviche ingredients in a medium bowl, and toss well. Serve with tortilla chips.

"When you want something, all the universe conspires in helping you to achieve it." Paulo Coelho

Beautifully Roasted Broccoli

This simple, healthfully alluring side dish can strengthen the body's defenses, making your system roused and more robust. Fresh green foods stimulate detoxification and signify renewal.

Serves 2-4

1 lb. broccoli, cut into florets
4 cloves garlic, sliced
3 tbsp. extra-light olive oil, divided

Salt
2 tbsp. grated Parmesan cheese
1 tbsp. dried parsley

Preheat oven to 425 degrees.

Place the broccoli on a large baking sheet in a single layer. Add the sliced garlic, 2 tbsp. oil, and a sprinkle of salt to taste. Bake for 15–20 minutes, stirring halfway through.

Transfer roasted broccoli to a bowl. Immediately add the remaining oil, the Parmesan, and the parsley. Toss well.

"Every decision you make stems from what you think you are, and represents the value you put upon yourself."
A Course in Miracles

Rosemary-Roasted Veggies

Rosemary's purifying properties and piney flavor make it a beautiful match for roasted veggies. This low-maintenance mix can be served as a simple side, and it also sets you up for a Roasted Veggie Wrap (see index).

Serves 2-4

8 oz. baby portobello mushrooms
1 red onion, cut into chunks
1 red bell pepper, cut into chunks
1 zucchini, sliced

1 tbsp. extra-light olive oil
1 tbsp. chopped fresh rosemary
Salt and freshly ground black pepper

Preheat oven to 400 degrees.

Lay the vegetables on a large, foil-lined baking sheet. Add the oil, rosemary, and salt and freshly ground black pepper to taste. Toss well to coat, and then arrange the veggies in a single layer.

Bake for 15 minutes. Shake the veggies around and drain the liquid out of the pan. Bake for 15 minutes more.

"So many of us choose our path out of fear disguised as practicality." Jim Carrey

Mashed Cauliflower

This light and fluffy alternative to mashed potatoes is pure, soft, and sprightly. You won't even miss the gravy.

Serves 2-4

1 head cauliflower, cut into florets
2-3 cloves garlic, pressed
1 tbsp. extra-virgin olive oil (plus extra
    for garnish)

Salt and freshly ground black pepper

Pour about 2 inches of water into a large pot and place a steamer basket inside. Bring the water to a boil, and then add the cauliflower florets to the basket. Reduce the heat to low and cover the pot. Cook the cauliflower for 12–15 minutes, until soft.

In a food processor, combine the cauliflower with the garlic, oil, and a sprinkle of salt to taste. Pulse until smooth and creamy. Add salt as needed.

Top each serving with freshly ground black pepper to taste and perhaps an extra drizzle of oil.

"Everything I've ever worried about in my whole life turned out OK. Funny that." Roger Rippy

Fish and Freshness

This lively dish is well balanced and clean, making all of its radiance easy to absorb. Eating fish in moderation is physically and mentally strengthening. Opt for high-quality wild-caught filets.

Serves 2

½ cup uncooked brown rice
2 plum tomatoes, chopped
½ cup chopped red onion
1 small yellow squash, sliced
Juice of 2 lemons

Salt and freshly ground black pepper
Olive oil cooking spray
2 (8 oz.) tilapia filets
¼ cup cilantro leaves
⅓ cup sliced pitted kalamata olives

Preheat oven to 425 degrees.

Prepare rice according to package directions.

Combine the tomatoes, red onion, squash, lemon juice, and salt and freshly ground black pepper to taste in a medium bowl. Toss well.

Each piece of fish will cook with veggies in an individual, foil-wrapped packet (you will need 6-8 large sheets of aluminum foil). Layer 3-4 large sheets of foil (per piece of fish). Coat each top sheet with cooking spray, and lay a piece of fish on top. Lightly salt both sides, then evenly divide the veggie mixture over the filets.

Enclose the fish in the foil. Make sure the seams are pinched together so no steam can get out, but don't make it too tight—allow some space between the veggies and foil. Bake for 25-30 minutes, depending on the thickness of the fish. To check doneness, insert a fork into the center of 1 filet (be careful—the foil tents are hot!). It should be white and flaky.

Carefully place the fish/veggies over the rice in shallow bowls. Top with cilantro and kalamata olives.

"Make your life about love. Love for you. Love for your higher power. And love for others. Give away what you want to receive. Make your life a demonstration of love." **Mastin Kipp**

Cherry Jam

"Chia" is the ancient Mayan word for "strength." This cleansing and filling spread will boost your energy and simultaneously help you sleep (thanks to the melatonin in the cherries).

Makes about ½ cup

1 cup frozen dark cherries, defrosted
1 tbsp. water

1 tbsp. chia seeds
Honey or agave (optional)

In a blender, lightly pulse the cherries and water for just a moment. Pour the mixture into a small container and stir in the chia. Let the mixture stand for 1 hour to thicken.

If you prefer a sweeter jam, stir in honey or agave to taste.

"It is through your body that you realize you are a spark of divinity." B. K. S. Iyengar

Kiddie Smoothie

This mindfully balanced, leafy-green smoothie is as delicious as it is nutritious. The peanut butter offers a hint of creamy decadence; milk and banana add smoothness; spinach and strawberries cleanse and awaken. This rejuvenating blend is a great snack, especially post-workout!

Serves 1

1 peeled banana, preferably frozen
1¼ cups spinach or kale
1 tbsp. peanut butter (optional)

3-4 frozen strawberries
1 cup unsweetened almond milk (plus
  extra as needed)

Combine all ingredients in a blender, and pulse until liquefied. Add more milk as necessary.

"When you release people, you allow them to show up in the way that they are meant to show up." Gabrielle Bernstein

Minty Banana-Kale Smoothie

Fresh mint and frozen pineapple make this vibrant green drink cool and refreshing, while the almond milk makes it grounding and well balanced. With the detoxifying qualities of leafy greens, the soothing banana, and pineapple's punch of vitamin C, this recipe is a go-to if you're stressed out!

Serves 1

1 ¼ cups kale (stems removed)
1 banana, peeled
⅓ cup frozen chopped pineapple

⅓ cup loosely packed mint leaves
1 ¼ cups unsweetened almond milk

Combine all the ingredients in a blender and pulse until liquefied.

"Get people back into the kitchen and combat the trend toward processed food and fast food." Andrew Weil

Minty Watermelon Refresher

This easy-to-digest, energizing pink drink artfully combines hydrating watermelon with soothing mint—a mix that can flush out the old and softly renew.

Serves 2

1 cup loosely packed mint
3 cups cubed watermelon
1 cup water

1 handful ice (about 4 cubes)
Fresh mint for garnish

Using a mortar and pestle, grind the mint for about 1 minute, until it is bright green, fragrant, and significantly reduced in volume. Discard the leaves and transfer the liquid extract (about 1 tbsp.) to a blender. Add the watermelon, water, and ice. Blend thoroughly.

"We need women who are so strong they can be gentle, so educated they can be humble, so fierce they can be compassionate, so passionate they can be rational, and so disciplined they can be free." Kavita Ramdas

Lemon-Aid

This may not be the most sophisticated concoction, but it is very refreshing. I have a glass almost every morning! Lemons increase enzyme activity and stimulate your liver. They flush out toxins, enhance digestion, boost your immunity, and consequently can improve your mood! Limes are great for this too.

Serves 1

¼ lemon
12 oz. water

Squeeze the juice from the lemon into a tall glass. Top it off with the water.

"The gift of intuition comes to those who practice with patience." Ana Forrest

feel Peaceful

Feel soothed and even-keeled.

Experience being gently uplifted.

This chapter is another source of wholesome dishes. Recipes here contain slightly heartier ingredients, but they are still largely light and nutritious. Within these pages you will find beans, vegetables, low-fat proteins, and whole grains, flavorfully combined to offer sustainable energy and guiltless satisfaction. The fresh ingredients and bulk of certain extra items (hello, cheese and pasta) will leave you feeling calm and light yet fulfilled and undeprived.

Purely Pea Soup

This sassy soup may look a little murky, but she's got it where it counts! Pea soup is a nerve-calming, immunity-boosting blend that is cleanly filling and packed with flavor. Ideally, prepare this soup a day in advance—it gets even richer, thicker, and more delicious as it sits.

Serves 4

2 tbsp. extra-virgin olive oil
1 onion, chopped
6 cloves garlic, minced
½ tsp. cumin
¼ tsp. dried thyme leaves

½ tsp. cayenne pepper
Salt and freshly ground black pepper
1 lb. bag dried peas, rinsed
32 oz. vegetable broth
1½ cups water

In a large pot or Dutch oven, heat the oil over medium heat. Add the onion, garlic, cumin, thyme, cayenne, and salt to taste. Let the mixture cook, stirring frequently, for 4–5 minutes.

Add the peas, broth, and water. Bring the mixture to a boil, and then reduce the heat, cover, and simmer for 1 hour.

Top each serving with freshly ground black pepper to taste.

"Let yourself be drawn by the stronger pull of that which you truly love." Rumi

Broccoli-Cheddar-White Bean Soup

Broccoli brightens you up, while the grounding nature of beans and cheese gently tempers its effects. As the broccoli cooks in this soup, its health-promoting properties are retained and it becomes easier to digest.

Serves 2

3 cups vegetable broth
1 lb. broccoli crowns, chopped (about 5 cups)
Salt
1 can cannellini beans, drained and rinsed

1 cup shredded cheddar cheese (plus extra for garnish)
Freshly ground black pepper

In a large pot, bring the broth to a boil. Add the broccoli and a sprinkle of salt to taste. Simmer the mixture, covered, for 10 minutes, until tender.

Add the beans and cook for 2 minutes. Stir in the cheese until it's melted.

Puree the soup with an immersion blender, or standard blender in batches, until it's creamy but still slightly textured.

Top each serving with freshly ground black pepper to taste and extra cheese as desired.

"The key to growth is the introduction of higher dimensions of consciousness into our awareness." Lao-Tzu

Roasted Red Pepper Soup

This highly nutritious, brightly colored soup draws upon the natural sweetness and textures of fresh ingredients. The finished product is beautiful, crowd-pleasing, and delicious.

Serves 4-6

3 red bell peppers
2-4 tbsp. extra-virgin olive oil, divided
1 onion, diced
5 cloves garlic, minced
2 large carrots, unpeeled but scrubbed and chopped
1 large potato, unpeeled but scrubbed and chopped

1 ripe pear, peeled and chopped
32 oz. vegetable broth
2 tbsp. chopped fresh parsley
Salt and pepper
Grated Parmesan cheese

Preheat oven to 400 degrees.

Lay the peppers on a foil-lined baking sheet. Bake for 20 minutes, then flip them over. Bake for 20 more minutes.

Place the peppers in a bowl and cover with a dish to seal in the steam. Let stand for 15-20 minutes, then remove and discard the stems, skins, and seeds.

In a large pot, heat 2 tbsp. oil over medium heat. Add the onions and garlic and cook for 4-5 minutes, stirring often.

Add the red peppers, carrots, and potato. Cook for 10 minutes, stirring often. Add more oil as necessary.

Add the pear, broth, and parsley. Bring the soup to a boil. Reduce the heat, cover, and simmer for 20 minutes, until the vegetables are tender.

Puree the soup using an immersion blender, or standard blender in batches, until it's mixed but still textured,. Reheat soup as necessary. Top each serving with salt, freshly ground black pepper, and Parmesan to taste.

"Stop dieting, listen to your body. Really listen to your body, not your mind . . . what your body wants to eat, when it wants to eat it and what feels good in your body." Geneen Roth

Zesty Kale Chips

These exciting chips are addictive. Unlike your average chip, they do not leave you feeling guilty and heavy. They are gently dehydrated, resulting in a deep flavor and perfect crunch. They'll fill you up too.

Serves 4

½ cup raw cashews
I cup water
½ red bell pepper
I lemon, peeled and seeded
2 green onions

5-6 baby carrots
2 cloves garlic, peeled
I tsp. apple cider vinegar
I tsp. salt
I bunch kale

Soak the cashews in 1 cup water for 2-4 hours.

Preheat oven to lowest heat setting, or "warm," if that's an option.

Drain the cashews and discard the water. Combine the cashews, red pepper, lemon, green onions, carrots, garlic, vinegar, and salt in a food processor, and pulse until smooth.

Remove stems from the kale and tear the leaves into bite-size pieces. In a large bowl, gently toss the kale leaves in the cashew mixture, coating them thoroughly.

Arrange the kale in a single layer over foil-lined baking sheets. Place them in the warm oven for 90 minutes. Use a spatula to flip the kale pieces over (they will likely be quite soggy). Continue to cook for 4-5 hours, until dry and crispy.

"Every problem has a gift for you in its hands." Richard Bach

Creamy-Ranchy Cashew Dip

Dip lovers, delight! This creamy, zesty, and all-natural spread is perfection with fresh veggies. Lemon juice and healthy fats add both nutrition and pizazz.

Makes about 1 cup

1 cup raw cashews
1⅓ cups water, divided
Juice of 1 lemon
1-2 cloves garlic

¼ tsp. dried dill
¼ tsp. dried oregano
1 tsp. salt
Veggies and/or crackers for serving

Soak the cashews in 1 cup water for 30 minutes or up to 4 hours. Discard the water and place the nuts in a food processor. Add the lemon juice, garlic, dill, oregano, and salt. For best results, start blending while slowly adding the ⅓ cup water. Blend for 2–3 minutes, until smooth and creamy.

Serve with veggies and/or crackers.

"Don't let what used to be a miracle become ordinary."
Joel Osteen

Tomato Bruschetta

Vine-ripened tomatoes and freshly picked basil make this beautiful bruschetta taste like a summertime treat. While tomatoes have refreshing effects, the bread, oil, and cheese are grounding, making for a calming combination.

Serves 6-8

5 cups diced tomatoes (8-10 tomatoes)
¾ cup chopped fresh basil
1 tbsp. extra-virgin olive oil
Salt and freshly ground black pepper
5-7 cloves garlic, peeled and halved
   lengthwise

1 baguette (11 oz.), thinly sliced and
   lightly toasted
½ cup shaved Parmesan cheese
   (optional)

In a medium bowl, mix the tomatoes, basil, and oil. Season with salt and freshly ground black pepper to taste. Set aside.

Rub the garlic cloves into both sides of the toasted bread. Spoon the tomato mixture onto the bread slices. Top with shaved Parmesan as desired.

"It's not always rainbows and butterflies, it's compromise that moves us along." **Maroon 5**

Spinach and Tomato Toast

This toast is worth a toast. Just as spinach strengthened Popeye, it will give you a boost here. With that said, cooking the leaves, and adding salt and oil, softly subdues that effect. This dish is especially soothing with hot soup on the side.

Serves 2

1 cup chopped tomato
3 tsp. extra-virgin olive oil, divided
1 tsp. dried basil
Salt
2 slices sprouted bread

1 clove garlic, peeled and halved
   lengthwise
2½ cups loosely packed baby spinach
Freshly ground black pepper

In a small bowl, combine the tomato, 1 tsp. oil, basil, and salt to taste. Stir well and set aside.

Toast the bread, and then rub the garlic clove into 1 side of each slice.

In a skillet, heat the remaining 2 tsp. oil over medium heat. Add the spinach and a pinch of salt. Cook, stirring often, for 3–5 minutes, until the leaves are bright green, wilted, and significantly reduced.

Lay the sautéed spinach over the toast. Spoon the tomato mixture on top, and add freshly ground black pepper to taste.

"People create their own questions because they are afraid to look straight. All you have to do is look straight and see the road, and when you see it, don't sit looking at it—walk."

Ayn Rand

Avocado Toast

Enjoy this as a Mediterranean-style breakfast or light lunch. Avocados make a wonderful spread that's filling and way better than butter! Flax oil is linked with mental clarity, calmness, and self-control. Who couldn't use some help with that?

Serves 2

1 avocado, peeled and mashed
2 slices sesame sprouted bread,
   toasted

1 tsp. flax oil
¼ tsp. chia seeds (optional)
Salt

Spread half of the mashed avocado over each slice of toasted bread. Top each with ½ tsp. oil, some chia seeds (if using), and salt to taste.

"Do what you can, with what you have, where you are."
Theodore Roosevelt

Italian White Bean Salad

Here is simplicity at its best. The buttery beans, blended with other delicious flavors, will fill you up in a powerfully cleansing way.

Serves 2-4

1 (15 oz.) can white beans, rinsed and drained
1 small clove garlic, minced
¼ cup chopped sundried tomatoes in oil, drained and oil reserved
¼ cup capers, drained
¼ cup diced red onion
1 tbsp. chopped fresh rosemary
Salt and freshly ground black pepper to taste

Place all the ingredients in a medium bowl, including 1 tbsp. reserved oil.

Use your hands to mix the ingredients and slightly crush the beans (this enhances the texture and melds the flavors).

For best results, make the salad a day in advance and serve it at room temperature, topped with freshly ground black pepper.

"In the midst of the deepest darkest night, act as if morning has already come." The Talmud

French Tuna Salad

This pretty salad makes for a perfect lunch or simple supper. It is a rejuvenating combination of vital greens, hearty potatoes, healthy fats, and lean, empowering protein. The earthy presentation inspires peaceful vibes.

Serves 4

1 lb. small white potatoes, quartered
1 lb. green beans, ends trimmed
⅓ cup extra-virgin olive oil
2 tbsp. Dijon mustard
2 tbsp. lemon juice
2 tsp. sugar
1¼ cups green olives with pimentos, divided

1⅓ cups arugula
1 avocado, peeled and chopped
1 (12 oz.) can solid white tuna, drained
¼ cup chopped fresh parsley
Freshly ground black pepper

Place the potatoes in a pot and add water to cover. Bring the mixture to a boil. Reduce the heat, cover, and simmer for 5 minutes.

Add the green beans. Simmer for another 5 minutes, until the potatoes are just tender. Drain and set aside.

To make the dressing, place the oil, Dijon, lemon juice, sugar, and 1 cup olives in a blender. Pulse until smooth.

Distribute the arugula over 4 plates (⅓ cup per plate). On top of the leaves, place small piles of potato, beans, avocado, tuna (in chunks), parsley, and remaining olives. Drizzle the dressing on top, and add freshly ground black pepper to taste.

"Don't be afraid of the space between your dreams and reality. If you can dream it, you can make it so." Belva Davis

Veggie Pockets

Creamy brie ties this lively sandwich together and makes the sautéed veggies especially spectacular! Grounded by the pita, the combination is harmonious and delicious.

Serves 6

3 tbsp. extra-virgin olive oil
1 onion, diced
4 cloves garlic, minced
1 bell pepper, diced
1 cup chopped mushrooms
½ crown broccoli, chopped (about 2 cups)

1 cup chopped zucchini
1 tsp. oregano
Salt
6 medium whole-wheat pita pockets
¼ lb. brie, cut into slices

Heat the oil over medium heat in a large skillet. Add the onion and garlic and cook, stirring frequently, for 4–5 minutes. Add the remaining veggies, oregano, and salt to taste. Continue to cook and stir occasionally, for about 10 minutes.

Cut the pitas in half crosswise. Lay a few slices of brie inside each half (if the pitas are too flimsy, use them in a way that resembles tacos instead of filling them). Gently spoon the veggie mixture over the brie.

"To me, faith is not worrying." John Dewey

Roasted Veggie Wrap

This bright, rosemary-infused wrap is potently flavorful. Packed with fresh ingredients, it is a great workweek lunch that won't have you slumping by two o'clock. For a lighter version, use collard wraps instead.

Serves 1

1 tbsp. hummus
1 spinach wrap
1 tbsp. crumbled feta cheese
1 cup Rosemary-Roasted Veggies (see index)

⅓ cup lettuce
⅓ cup alfalfa sprouts
½ avocado, peeled and sliced

Spread the hummus in a long line down the center of the wrap. Distribute the feta on top, and then lay on the roasted veggies, lettuce, and sprouts. Place avocado slices on top. Tuck in the ends of the wrap and gently roll it up. Slice in half crosswise.

"Folks are like plants; we all lean toward the light." **Kris Carr**

Smoked Salmon Sandwiches

This deceptively simple sandwich is salty, sweet, meaty, and delicate all at the same time. The texture is a perfectly balanced combination of dilly cream cheese, soft salmon, and crunchy cucumbers.

Serves 2

8 oz. smoked salmon
½ cucumber, thinly sliced
1 small tomato, sliced

4 slices pumpernickel bread
2 tbsp. cream cheese
2 tsp. dried dill

Divide the salmon, cucumber, and tomato over 2 slices of bread. In a small bowl, combine the cream cheese and dill. Spread the mixture over the remaining 2 slices of bread.

Place the cheesy slices over the salmon and veggies. Cut in half.

"What is necessary to change a person is to change his awareness of himself." Abraham Maslow

Sprouted Collard Wraps

Roasted veggies and a thin layer of hummus make these collard wraps intriguing and unique. Leafy greens are crucial for detoxification. Paired here with other superfoods, they will help you feel calm yet bright.

Serves 4

12-16 oz. Brussels sprouts, cut in half
1 small head cauliflower, broken into florets
¼ cup extra-light olive oil
Salt

1 bunch collard greens
1 cup loosely packed alfalfa sprouts
1 tomato, diced
1 avocado, peeled and sliced
½ cup hummus

Preheat oven to 400 degrees.

On a large baking sheet, toss the Brussels sprouts and cauliflower with the oil and salt to taste. Bake for 35–40 minutes, shaking the sheet every 10 minutes.

Cut the thick stems and spines out of the collards. Depending on how sturdy the leaves are, there are different ways to make your wraps.

Option 1: Lay out 1 leaf (bright-green side facing down). In a thin line, spread a small handful of Brussels sprouts and cauliflower and then some alfalfa sprouts, tomato, and avocado. Carefully roll up the leaf, and just before it's completely closed, spread a line of hummus. Close the wrap and insert a toothpick to hold it together. Repeat the process with the remaining leaves.

Option 2 (if the leaves are more flimsy): Take 1 leaf and fold it in half lengthwise (bright-green side facing out). In a thin line, spread a small handful of Brussels sprouts and cauliflower and then some alfalfa sprouts, tomato, and avocado. Carefully roll up the leaf, and just before it's completely closed, spread a line of hummus. Close the wrap and insert a toothpick to hold it together. Repeat the process with the remaining leaves.

"[Love] keeps no record of being wronged." 1 Corinthians 13:5

Super Spaghetti Squash

This colorful side/main dish is even more fantastic than the sum of its potently flavorful parts. Subtly sweet squash is brought to life by herbs, olives, feta, and artichokes, while the chopped tomatoes add juiciness and a mellower vibe.

Serves 4

I medium spaghetti squash
⅓ cup sliced pitted kalamata olives
I cup chopped artichoke hearts from a
   can or jar, rinsed and drained
¼ cup chopped fresh basil
½ cup chopped fresh parsley

3 tbsp. extra-virgin olive oil
Salt and freshly ground black pepper
   to taste
3 tomatoes, diced
⅔ cup crumbled feta cheese

Preheat oven to 375 degrees.

Slice the squash in half lengthwise. Scoop out the seeds, and place it cut side down on a foil-lined baking sheet. Bake for 35–45 minutes. Once it has cooled, use a fork to scrape the spaghetti-like flesh into a large pot or Dutch oven. Discard the skin. Add the remaining ingredients, except the feta cheese, and heat the mixture over medium heat, stirring frequently. Lightly stir the feta in before serving. Top with freshly ground black pepper.

"Courage is doing what you're afraid to do. There can be no courage unless you're scared." Eddie Rickenbacker

Roasted Brussels Sprouts

These tender and slightly caramelized sprouts melt in your mouth. With their addictive saltiness and oily feel, you may find yourself downing them like popcorn (but you will feel much better later!).

Serves 2

1 lb. Brussels sprouts, cut in half
2 tbsp. extra-light olive oil
Salt

Preheat oven to 400 degrees.

On a large baking sheet, toss the sprouts with the oil and salt to taste. Bake for 30–35 minutes, shaking the sheet every 10 minutes.

"An undisciplined mind, easily tempted into faithless and unloving thoughts, is a huge deterrent to success." Marianne Williamson

Fava Beans with Parsley

Fava beans work well with parsley, cumin, and red onion in this slightly sweet and cleansing side dish that can easily be featured as an entree. Cumin improves circulation, red onion purifies, and parsley helps you to digest the beans. Oh, and this tastes great too.

Serves 4-6

9 tbsp. extra-virgin olive oil, divided
2 cups diced red onion
Salt
6 slices high-quality bread
3 cloves garlic, peeled and halved
　lengthwise

1 tbsp. cumin
1 (19 oz.) can fava beans, rinsed and
　drained
1 cup chopped fresh parsley, divided
Freshly ground black pepper

In a large skillet, heat 3 tbsp. oil over medium heat. Add the onion and salt to taste, and cook for 10 minutes, stirring frequently.

In the meantime, toast the bread. Rub the garlic cloves into both sides of each slice.

Stir the cumin into the onions, then add the fava beans. Cook for 2 minutes more. Add ¼ cup parsley. Stir and remove the pan from the heat.

Spoon a heaping pile of the bean mixture over each slice of garlic toast. Drizzle 1 tbsp. oil on top, then add salt and freshly ground black pepper to taste and a generous handful of parsley.

"Telling the truth is not just what you say, it's how you show up. It's being the Truth." India.Arie

Rice and Beans

This uniquely textured, fiber-rich dish will fill you up and clean you out! The beans, garlic, and splash of hot sauce offer heat, while the raw toppings promote a peaceful balance.

Serves 4

1 cup uncooked brown basmati rice	1 cup canned fat-free refried beans
2 tbsp. extra-virgin olive oil	2 tbsp. hot sauce
1 onion, diced	4 small tomatoes, diced, divided
3-4 cloves garlic, minced	1 avocado, peeled and chopped
1 (15 oz.) can black beans, rinsed and drained	Shredded cheddar cheese (optional)
	Jarred jalapeno slices (optional)

Cook the rice according to package directions.

In the meantime, in a separate medium pot, heat the oil over medium heat. Add the onion and garlic, and cook for 4–5 minutes, stirring often.

Stir in the black and refried beans and cook for 3–5 minutes, until the refried beans thin out. Add the hot sauce and half of the chopped tomatoes. Cook for a few more minutes until the mixture is heated through.

To serve, layer the bean mixture over the rice in individual bowls. Top each serving with tomatoes and chopped avocado. Add shredded cheddar cheese and jalapeno slices as desired.

"Your relationship to food is a reflection of your relationship to yourself, as is everything in your life." Marianne Williamson

Turkey Chili

This lean yet hearty main dish is wholesome and satisfying. It's a one-pot meal that's easy to whip up and clean up! If you like extra spice, mince a small jalapeno and add it in with the onion and garlic, and/or use more cayenne. Doing so can help you feel fuller for longer and increase metabolism too.

Serves 4-6

I tbsp. olive oil	I can black beans, rinsed and drained
I large onion, diced	2 tsp. ground cumin
6 garlic cloves, minced	2 tbsp. chili powder
I red bell pepper, diced	½ tsp. oregano
Salt	½ tsp. cayenne
I lb. ground turkey	Shredded cheddar cheese
2 (14.5 oz.) cans diced tomatoes	I avocado, peeled and chopped
2 tbsp. tomato paste	¼ cup chopped cilantro
I can kidney beans, rinsed and drained	Jarred jalapeno slices

Heat the oil in a large skillet over medium heat. Add the onion, garlic, red pepper, and a few sprinkles of salt to taste. Cook for about 10 minutes, and then add the turkey. Cook for 5 minutes more, stirring often, until brown.

Stir in the diced tomatoes and tomato paste. Add the beans, cumin, chili powder, oregano, and cayenne. Bring the mixture to a boil. Reduce heat, cover, and simmer for 30 minutes, stirring occasionally. Add salt to taste.

For best results, make the chili a day or two in advance so the flavors can meld. Refrigerate and then reheat to serve. Top each serving with cheese, avocados, cilantro, and jalapenos.

"Many people have lost touch with their inner voice, or the Tao within, and they consequently live against the grain of their own being, experiencing much suffering as a result."
Mantak Chia and William U. Wei

Perfect Pasta Primavera

In this pretty primavera, the veggies are roasted just long enough for them to soften and their natural sweetness to come through. Tossed with pasta, oil, and cheese, this fresh dish is superbly satisfying at the same time.

Serves 6

2 medium zucchini, cut into semicircles

4 medium yellow squash, cut into semicircles

3 carrots, unpeeled but scrubbed and cut into strips

1 can chickpeas, drained and rinsed

1 onion, thinly sliced

2 cloves garlic, minced

2 bell peppers (any color), thinly sliced

¼ cup extra-light olive oil

Salt

1 tbsp. Italian seasoning

12 oz. whole-wheat rotini

10 oz. cherry tomatoes, halved

½ cup grated Parmesan cheese

Extra-virgin olive oil for garnish

Freshly ground black pepper

Dried parsley for garnish

Preheat oven to 450 degrees.

Place the zucchini, squash, carrots, chickpeas, onion, garlic, and peppers in a large bowl, and add the extra-light olive oil, salt to taste, and Italian seasoning. Toss well. Spread the mixture over 2 baking sheets. Bake for 25 minutes, stirring halfway through.

In the meantime, cook the pasta in salted water, according to package directions. Reserve 1 cup of the cooking water before draining.

Return the cooked vegetables to the large bowl. Lay the tomato halves over 1 of the hot baking sheets. Broil them for 1-2 minutes, until they are warm and slightly broken down.

Add the pasta, reserved cooking water, broiled tomatoes, and Parmesan to the large bowl with the vegetables. Toss well.

Drizzle each serving with extra-virgin olive oil, then sprinkle with salt and freshly ground black pepper to taste and dried parsley.

"It is good to love many things, for therein lies true strength, and whosoever loves much performs much, and can accomplish much, and what is done in love is well done."

Vincent Van Gogh

Pasta with Greens

Pasta, meet salad. In this bright and nutritious dish, spaghetti is a vessel for whole bunches of leafy greens. The combination is restoratively soothing.

Serves 4

12-16 oz. whole-wheat spaghetti
1 bunch rainbow chard
3 tbsp. extra-virgin olive oil
4 cloves garlic, minced
1 tsp. salt
1 tsp. red pepper flakes (plus extra for garnish)

1 bunch spinach, roughly chopped
1 cup water
2 tbsp. tomato paste
½ cup freshly shaved Parmesan (plus extra for garnish)
Freshly ground black pepper

Prepare the spaghetti in salted water according to package directions. Reserve ½ cup cooking water and set aside.

Separate the stems from the chard greens. Roughly chop the chard greens, and then roughly chop the stems. Set each aside.

In a large pot, heat the olive oil over medium heat. Add the garlic, chopped chard stems, salt, and red pepper flakes. Cook for about 1 minute, stirring often. Add the chard greens and spinach, and stir frequently for 2-3 minutes, until they are cooked down and wilted.

Stir 1 cup water and tomato paste into the pot. Bring to a boil, then reduce heat, cover, and simmer for 5-10 minutes.

Stir the cooked spaghetti, Parmesan, and ½ cup reserved pasta water into the pot.

Top each serving with freshly ground black pepper, red pepper flakes, and extra Parmesan cheese to taste.

"A deep social connection, the breadth and depth and the meaning in our relationships, is one of the greatest predictors of long-term levels of happiness we have." Shawn Achor

Simple Tuna Pasta

Fresh herbs add intrigue and stimulate digestion in this straightforward and satisfying dish. Pasta rounds out the recipe and easily makes it a meal.

Serves 4

1 cup whole-wheat elbow pasta
1 (5 oz.) can solid white tuna in
   water, drained
4 medium tomatoes, diced
1 cup chopped spinach
¼ cup capers, drained

¾ cup chopped artichokes from a can
   or jar, rinsed and drained
2 tbsp. chopped fresh basil
2 tbsp. chopped fresh parsley
2 tbsp. extra-virgin olive oil
Salt and freshly ground black pepper

Cook the pasta according to package directions.

In a separate bowl, mix the tuna, tomatoes, spinach, capers, artichokes, basil, and parsley. Add the pasta and oil to the tuna mixture. Season with salt and freshly ground black pepper to taste and toss well.

"If we want to make meaning, we need to make art. Cook, write, draw, doodle, paint, scrapbook, take pictures, collage, knit, rebuild an engine, sculpt, dance, decorate, act, sing—it doesn't matter. As long as we're creating, we're cultivating meaning." Brene Brown

Orzo and Arugula Salad

Potent arugula is complemented by other lively ingredients in this bright and satisfying salad. The pasta adds substance to make it more of a meal.

Serves 4-6

⅔ cup uncooked orzo pasta
1 cup chopped arugula
1 cup chopped lettuce
1 cup diced tomatoes
⅔ cup diced red bell pepper
¼ cup diced red onion
¼ cup shaved carrot

⅓ cup chopped fresh basil
1 small cooked rotisserie chicken
1 tbsp. extra-virgin olive oil
2 tbsp. red-wine vinegar
Salt
⅓ cup crumbled feta cheese
Freshly ground black pepper

Cook the orzo according to package directions. Drain and set aside.

In the meantime, in a large bowl, combine all the veggies with the meat from the chicken. Add the orzo when it's ready. Add the oil, vinegar, and salt to taste, and toss well to coat. Top with feta cheese and freshly ground black pepper to taste.

"The sexiest thing in the entire world is being really smart and being thoughtful, and being generous. Everything else is crap."
Ashton Kutcher

feel Comforted

Feel warm and satisfied.

Enjoy feeling softly subdued.

Comfort foods are exactly what they sound like. Here are warm, satisfying dishes that will leave you feeling contentedly nourished and snugly at home. These are not low-calorie recipes. They are hearty, saucy, cheesy, and sometimes heavy.

Comfort foods are especially suited for cold nights and wintry weather. Eaten in moderation, they are inviting and filling, but when they are overdone, they will bloat and disrupt your system. Tune in to *feel* for your comfy balance!

Hearty Breakfast Strata

Dense and delicious, this is my family's Christmas-morning breakfast tradition. It is a filling blend of meat, veggies, cheese, and custardy bread. That's a holiday present all in itself.

Serves 8–10

1 loaf whole-wheat baguette, cut into
  1-inch slices
5 eggs
1 tsp. Dijon mustard
1 tsp. dried basil
½ tsp. salt
1½ cups half-and-half
2 cups grated sharp cheddar cheese,
  divided

1 green bell pepper, chopped
1 pt. cherry tomatoes, cut into
  quarters
1 onion, diced
1 (9.6 oz.) pkg. breakfast sausage,
  cooked and cut into ¼-inch slices
1 tbsp. dried parsley

Grease a 9x13 baking pan. Lay the bread slices along the bottom. If you have some leftover bread, rip those pieces up and tuck them in to cover the entire bottom of the dish.

Combine the eggs, Dijon, basil, and salt. Whisk in the half-and-half. Pour the mixture over the bread. Use your hands to press the pieces down and get them wet. Cover the pan and refrigerate overnight (or at least 2 hours).

Preheat oven to 350 degrees.

Top the bread mixture with half of the cheese, then the veggies, sausage, remaining cheese, and parsley. Cover loosely with foil.

Bake for 20 minutes, and then remove the foil and bake 20 minutes more. Cool for 5 minutes.

"You must all be quick to listen, slow to speak, and slow to get angry." James 1:19

Roasted Asparagus with Goat Cheese and Eggs

This flavorful, well-rounded dish is best served in the first half of the day. While the asparagus boosts your energy and the eggs get your brain working, the rich and creamy goat cheese provides a sense of comfort.

Serves 2

1 cup chopped asparagus (1-2-inch pieces)
1 tsp. extra-virgin olive oil
½ tsp. rosemary
Salt
1 clove garlic, peeled and halved lengthwise

2 slices high-quality bread, toasted
4-6 tbsp. goat cheese
4 eggs
Freshly ground black pepper

Preheat oven to 450 degrees.

On a small baking sheet, toss the asparagus with the oil, rosemary, and a sprinkle of salt. Roast for 6–8 minutes.

In the meantime, rub the garlic clove into the toasted pieces of bread, and then evenly spread goat cheese on the tops.

To poach the eggs 2 at a time, bring a pot of water to a light boil. Crack 2 eggs into 2 small bowls or cups. Using a slotted spoon, stir the water in a circular motion to create a whirlpool effect. Gently lower 1 container into the water and release the egg. Do the same with the second container. Allow them to cook for 3 minutes. Remove the eggs with the slotted spoon and lay them over 1 slice cheesy bread. Pierce the yolks to let them run. Repeat with the remaining eggs.

Top with roasted asparagus, extra salt, and freshly ground black pepper to taste.

"If you cannot sing or laugh before a meal, skip it until you can." Mantak Chia and William U. Wei

Smoked-Salmon Eggs Benedict

Hold the heavy hollandaise. Salty salmon, crumbled feta, and fresh oregano give this radiant recipe its flavor. The dish offers strength and comfort in one fell swoop.

Serves 2

3 oz. smoked salmon
2 whole-wheat English muffins, sliced
   open and toasted
4 eggs

2 tbsp. crumbled feta cheese
2 tbsp. chopped fresh oregano
1 tsp. extra-virgin olive oil
Salt and freshly ground black pepper

Distribute the pieces of salmon atop all 4 pieces of toasted English muffin.

To poach the eggs 2 at a time, bring a pot of water to a light boil. Crack 2 eggs into 2 small bowls or cups. Using a slotted spoon, stir the water in a circular motion to create a whirlpool effect. Gently lower 1 container into the water and release the egg. Do the same with the second container. Allow them to cook for 3 minutes. Remove the eggs with the slotted spoon and place them atop the salmon on the English muffins. Pierce the yolks to let them run. Repeat with the remaining eggs.

Over the eggs, distribute the feta, oregano, oil, and salt and freshly ground black pepper to taste.

"You cannot have a positive life and a negative mind."
Joyce Meyer

Honey-Oat Granola

Homemade granola is more natural and often less sugary than the store-bought stuff. This eclectic version is sweet, crunchy, fiber rich, and filling. It goes beautifully with plain yogurt that's perhaps slightly sweetened with a few delicate drops of raw honey.

Makes about 3 cups

2 cups old-fashioned oats
¾ cup chopped or sliced almonds
2 tbsp. extra-light olive oil
¼ cup honey
2 tbsp. milled flax

2 tbsp. unsweetened coconut
2 tbsp. cocoa nibs or 1 square
   unsweetened cocoa, chopped
½ cup raisins

Preheat oven to 350 degrees. Grease a large baking sheet.

In a large bowl, combine all the ingredients except the raisins. Toss well to coat.

Spread the mixture on the baking sheet. Bake for 10 minutes, stirring halfway through.

After baking, let the granola cool on the sheet for 15 minutes. Add the raisins.

Store the granola in an airtight container. Serve as a dry snack, over yogurt, or in a bowl with milk.

"Fear is the path to the dark side." Yoda

Creamy Stuffed Mushrooms

This dish has rich ingredients and an indulgent vibe, but with redeeming nutritional value too! Mushrooms decrease blood lipids and reduce toxins associated with eating meat. Be careful, though—too many of these cheesy nibbles will leave you feeling stuffed and sluggish.

Serves 4

2 (8 oz.) pkg. baby portobello
  mushrooms
2 tbsp. water
2 cloves garlic, pressed
4 oz. goat cheese

2 tbsp. grated Parmesan cheese
10 pitted kalamata olives, chopped
¼ cup chopped sundried tomatoes
2 green onions, chopped

Preheat oven to 400 degrees.

Remove mushroom stems and set aside. Toss the mushroom caps with the water and pressed garlic. Transfer them to a baking sheet (open side up). Pour any remaining garlic liquid over the mushrooms. Bake for 8-10 minutes, until soft.

In the meantime, discard half of the mushroom stems. Finely chop the rest, and place them in a medium bowl. Add the goat cheese, Parmesan, olives, sundried tomatoes, and green onions. Stir well.

When the mushrooms come out of the oven, drop generous scoops of the cheese mixture into each cap. Return the stuffed mushrooms to the oven and bake for 5-10 minutes, until the cheese is warm.

"Love is, of all passions, the strongest, for it attacks simultaneously the head, the heart, and the senses." Lao-Tzu

Stuffed Portobellos with Balsamic Reduction

Meaty mushrooms and balsamic vinegar carry this dish, balanced by the comforting cushions of salt, oil, and cheese.

Serves 1-2

1 cup chopped baby spinach
1 tomato, diced
2 cloves garlic, pressed
Salt
1 tbsp. extra-virgin olive oil

2 large portobello mushrooms
¼ cup shredded mozzarella
¼ cup balsamic vinegar
Freshly ground black pepper

Preheat oven to 350 degrees.

Combine the spinach, tomato, garlic, salt to taste, and oil. Toss well. Spoon half of this mixture into the portobellos. Top with cheese. Add the remaining veggies on top. Bake for 20-25 minutes.

While the mushrooms bake, heat the balsamic in a small pot over medium heat. Once it starts to boil, reduce the heat and simmer for 8-10 minutes, until it reduces and thickens.

Pour the balsamic reduction (roughly 1 tbsp.) over the cooked portobellos. Top with freshly ground black pepper to taste.

"Listen to yourself and in that quietude you might hear the voice of God." Maya Angelou

Onion and Spinach Soup

Lighter than your average onion soup, this still-cheesy cup of comfort has added vitality, courtesy of 1 full container of spinach! Just as slicing onions can make you cry, eating them can stir up feelings as well. It's nothing to fear; each brothy bowl is warm and healing. You may experience a subtle catharsis.

Serves 8-10

¼ cup extra-virgin olive oil
5 large onions, thickly sliced
5 cloves garlic, minced
Salt
8 cups vegetable broth

5 oz. baby spinach
½ baguette, cut into ½-inch slices
8 oz. Gruyere cheese, grated
Freshly ground black pepper

Heat the oil in a large pot over medium-low heat. Add the onions, garlic, and a few sprinkles of salt. Cook for 30 minutes, stirring often.

Add the broth. Increase the heat to medium and bring the mixture to a boil. Then reduce the heat and simmer, covered, for 35 minutes. Stir in the spinach and simmer, covered, for 5 more minutes.

In the meantime, preheat the oven to 350 degrees.

Lay the bread slices on a baking sheet. Bake them for 5 minutes on each side, until lightly toasted.

Ladle the soup into oven-safe bowls. Add salt to taste. Top each with toasted bread and a handful of cheese.

Bake for 10 minutes, and then broil for 1-2 minutes, until the cheese is bubbly and lightly browned. Top each serving with freshly ground black pepper to taste.

"Soul is about authenticity. Soul is about finding the things in your life that are real and pure." John Legend

Herbed Garlic Potato Chips

White potatoes are calming when you're stressed! Prepared this flavorful way, with a lot of fresh garlic, spuds can fill you with comfort.

Serves 4-6

2 potatoes, scrubbed and thinly sliced   Salt
2-3 tbsp. extra-light olive oil   7+ cloves garlic, pressed, divided
2 tbsp. dried rosemary or oregano

Preheat oven to 450 degrees.

Combine the potatoes, oil, rosemary or oregano, salt to taste, and 3 cloves of pressed garlic in a large bowl. Toss well to coat.

Arrange the potatoes in a single layer over 2 or more baking sheets. Bake for 25-30 minutes, turning over the potatoes halfway through.

Over each serving, sprinkle a little extra salt and 1 clove pressed garlic.

"The ultimate measure of a man is not where he stands in moments of comfort and convenience, but where he stands at times of challenge and controversy." Dr. Martin Luther King, Jr.

Fiery Garlic Bread

Jalapeno and raw garlic make this cheesy bread a sizzling-hot source of carbs. It's portioned perfectly for 1-2 people, so it won't spoil your appetite.

Serves 1–2

1 large ciabatta roll or small piece baguette
1 tbsp. extra-virgin olive oil
2 cloves garlic, minced

8-10 jarred jalapeno slices
Salt
¼ cup shredded mozzarella
Dried parsley

Slice the bread open and lightly toast it.

Spread oil over the open-faced toast, then sprinkle garlic on top. Add the jalapeno slices, salt to taste, and mozzarella. Broil for 2 minutes, or until the cheese is bubbly and slightly brown (watch carefully to avoid burning). Top with dried parsley to taste.

"Laughter is carbonated holiness." **Anne Lamott**

Stuffed Broccoli Bread

Broccoli fights disease, boosts immunity, and produces radiance. This bread contains a whole bunch, and yet it tastes like a comforting treat.

Serves 6

1 bunch broccoli, finely chopped
(stems included)
1 tbsp. extra-virgin olive oil
1 tsp. salt
Flour

Fresh, raw pizza dough
6-8 cloves garlic, minced
6 oz. fresh mozzarella, sliced
Olive-oil cooking spray

Preheat oven to 350 degrees.

In a large bowl, toss the broccoli with the olive oil and salt. Transfer the mixture to a foil-lined baking sheet. Bake for 30 minutes.

Dust a clean countertop with some flour (to prevent sticking) and roll out the dough. Lay the cooked broccoli in a line through the center of the dough. Make sure it's narrow enough for the sides to eventually fold up to cover.

Distribute the garlic and mozzarella over the broccoli. Then fold the sides of the dough up and the ends in, to form a closed loaf. Spray the top with cooking spray.

Bake for 30 minutes directly on the oven rack, with a pan on the rack underneath (if the bread doesn't seem sturdy enough for this, bake it on a greased baking sheet instead). Use a towel to remove the bread from the oven.

"Those who bring sunshine to the lives of others cannot keep it from themselves." James Barrie

Packed Portobello Sandwiches

This seriously flavorful pile of goodness is fresh and bold. The meaty portobellos, tangy balsamic, and rich bleu cheese make the sandwich substantial, while there's just enough lightness (hello, spinach!) to balance it all out.

Serves 4

4 large portobello mushrooms, stems removed
6 tbsp. balsamic vinegar
2 tbsp. + 1 tsp. extra-virgin olive oil, divided
2 cloves garlic, pressed

1 red onion, sliced
8 slices high-quality bread or 4 rolls
8 strips roasted red pepper
4 small handfuls baby spinach
⅓ cup crumbled bleu cheese

Combine the mushrooms, vinegar, 2 tbsp. oil, and garlic in a large zip-top bag. Shake the bag so the mushrooms are well coated, then let them marinate for about 15 minutes.

In the meantime, sauté the red onion in the remaining 1 tsp. oil for about 10 minutes, stirring frequently.

Grill the mushrooms over indirect heat for about 5 minutes on each side.

To prepare each sandwich, lay a mushroom over 1 slice bread (consider slicing the mushrooms to make the sandwiches easier to eat). Top with some sautéed red onion, 2 strips roasted red pepper, 1 small handful spinach, and about 1 tbsp. bleu cheese. Add the top slice of bread.

"The end is inherent in the means." Mahatma Gandhi

Zucchini Rice

This creamy rice recipe pairs grounding whole grains with illuminating zucchini. Brown basmati soothes the stomach and calms the nerves, while zucchini lends lightness and moisture. Parmesan drives home the comfort.

Serves 6

1 tbsp. butter
¾ cup chopped onion
1 cup uncooked brown basmati rice
¼ tsp. fresh thyme
Salt

2¼ cups vegetable broth, divided
1 medium zucchini, shredded (about 1½ cups)
3 tbsp. Parmesan cheese

In a medium pot, melt the butter over medium heat. Add the onion and cook until soft, 4-5 minutes.

Add the rice, thyme, and salt to taste and stir well. Add 2 cups broth and bring the mixture to a boil. Reduce the heat and simmer, covered, for 20 minutes.

Stir the shredded zucchini and remaining ¼ cup broth into the pot. Continue to simmer, still covered, for 10 minutes more.

Stir in the Parmesan and add salt to taste. Remove from heat. If more liquid needs to be absorbed, let the mixture stand in the pot for a few minutes, uncovered.

"There is no passion to be found in settling for a life that is less than the one you are capable of living." Nelson Mandela

Spinach, Artichoke, and Mushroom Casserole

This nerve-relaxing dish is wonderful for a cold winter's night. It's a hearty, textured casserole that will make you feel warm, nourished, and supported.

Serves 6

1½ cups uncooked brown basmati rice
1 stick butter
1 onion, diced
¼ cup flour
Salt
1 cup milk
2 cups vegetable broth, divided
4 cups baby spinach

8 oz. baby portobello mushrooms, sliced
12 oz. artichoke hearts from a can or jar, rinsed and chopped
1 tbsp. dried parsley
½ cup slivered almonds
Freshly ground black pepper

Prepare the rice according to package directions.

Preheat oven to 425 degrees. Grease a 9x13 baking pan.

In a large pot, melt the butter over medium heat. Add the onion and cook for 3-4 minutes, until slightly soft. Add the flour and salt to taste. Stir in well. Slowly add the milk and 1 cup broth, stirring constantly until thick.

Add the spinach, mushrooms, artichokes, parsley, prepared rice, and remaining 1 cup broth. Stir continuously for 2-3 minutes, until the spinach cooks down.

Transfer the mixture to the baking pan. Top with slivered almonds.

Bake for 30 minutes. Let the casserole stand for 20-25 minutes before serving. Top each serving with freshly ground black pepper to taste.

"If you want others to be happy, practice compassion. If you want to be happy, practice compassion." Dalai Lama

Cheddar-Broccoli-Quinoa Casserole

Quinoa gives this creamy casserole a solid foundation, while broccoli gives it life. It is a cozy dish, especially when it's cool outside.

Serves 4

¾ cup uncooked quinoa
1¾ cups vegetable broth
½ lb. broccoli, chopped (about 2½ cups)
1 tbsp. flour

1 tbsp. butter
1 cup milk
1 cup shredded cheddar cheese, divided
Salt and freshly ground black pepper

Preheat oven to 350 degrees. Grease a medium casserole dish.

Combine the quinoa and broth in a medium pot. Bring to a boil. Reduce the heat, cover, and simmer for 10 minutes. Add the broccoli, and cook for 10 minutes more.

In the meantime, combine the flour and butter in a separate pot over medium heat. Stir for about 1 minute, until well combined, and then slowly pour in the milk. Raise the heat slightly and continue to stir frequently for 5–10 minutes, until thick. Turn off the heat and thoroughly stir in ½ cup cheese.

Add the quinoa mixture to the cheese sauce. Stir in salt and freshly ground black pepper to taste. Pour the mixture into the casserole dish. Top with remaining cheese. Bake for 15 minutes.

"The best way out is always through." Robert Frost

Garlic and Red Pepper Quinoa

This red-hot recipe packs a punch! Quinoa is a seed that imparts a sense of feeling rooted, while the pepper will lighten you up. It's a highly flavorful yet soothing combination.

Serves 2

½ cup quinoa

1 cup vegetable broth (plus extra as needed)

3 tbsp. seeded, finely chopped jalapeno

⅓ cup finely chopped red bell pepper

3-4 cloves garlic, minced

Salt to taste

¼ cup grated Parmesan cheese

Combine all the ingredients, except the Parmesan, in a medium pot. Bring the mixture to a boil. Then reduce the heat and simmer, covered, for 20 minutes, until the liquid is absorbed. Stir in the Parmesan. Add 3-4 tbsp. more broth if the mixture seems dry.

"The weak can never forgive. Forgiveness is an attribute of the strong." Mahatma Gandhi

Avocado-Jalapeno Pizza

Fresh avocado beautifies this pizza and works magic on your complexion as well. It's a harmonizing fruit that's considered brain food—a perfect match for jalapenos, which revitalize the lungs and open up internal energy. Still, the cheese and crust moderate these lively effects to leave you feeling comforted overall.

Serves 2

¾ cup pizza sauce
1 thin-crust whole-wheat pizza crust, such as Boboli
1¼ cups shredded mozzarella
1 clove garlic, minced

1 fresh jalapeno, sliced (remove seeds if you want to cut down on spiciness)
½ small red onion, sliced
3 tbsp. diced tomato
½ avocado, peeled and thinly sliced

Preheat oven to 450 degrees.

Spread the pizza sauce over the crust, then evenly distribute the cheese. Top with garlic, jalapeno, onion, and tomato.

Bake for 8–10 minutes, directly on the oven rack.

Spread the avocado slices over the pizza.

"When you show up and are willing to speak from your heart, come what may, that authenticity communicates directly with other people's hearts. Doing so creates an energy that inspires you and those around you." Baron Baptiste

Roasted Tomato and Garlic Pizza

Plum tomatoes caramelize to create a fabulous foundation in this radiant recipe. The cheesy, hearty pie is simple and yet substantial. Enjoy it with a salad on the side to lighten things up.

Serves 2

6-8 plum tomatoes, cut in half
6 cloves garlic, cut into quarters
3 tbsp. extra-light olive oil, divided
Salt
1 whole-wheat pizza crust, such as
  Boboli

8 oz. fresh mozzarella, sliced
1 small bunch fresh basil
2 tbsp. Parmesan cheese

Preheat oven to 350 degrees.

Lay the tomatoes and garlic on a baking sheet. Top with 2 tbsp. olive oil and salt to taste. Toss to coat. Bake for 20 minutes, and then stir. Bake an additional 30 minutes. Set aside.

Raise the oven temperature to 425 degrees.

Spread the tomato mixture over the crust. Top with the cheese slices, but rearrange some of the tomatoes to overlap the cheese. Add fresh basil leaves and sprinkle with Parmesan. Spoon the remaining olive oil over the top. Bake for 8–10 minutes.

"Ask not what you can do for your country. Ask what's for lunch." Orson Welles

Roasted Vegetable Quesadillas

These beautifully balanced quesadillas are stimulating and grounding at the same time. The jalapeno adds a fiery vibe, while the zucchini is more cooling and evokes a sense of calm. Cheese and tortillas bring it all together in a fun and comforting way!

Serves 2

1 red, yellow, or orange bell pepper, sliced
1 jalapeno, sliced (optional)
1 small zucchini, sliced
1 medium red onion, sliced
2 cloves garlic, minced
2 tbsp. extra-light olive oil
Salt
Olive-oil cooking spray
4 (8 inch) whole-wheat tortillas
1 cup shredded sharp cheddar cheese, divided

Preheat oven to 425 degrees.

On a large baking sheet, combine the pepper, jalapeno, zucchini, onion, garlic, olive oil, and salt to taste. Toss well to coat. Bake for 25 minutes, until the vegetables are lightly browned.

Divide the vegetables into fourths on the baking sheet.

Coat a medium skillet with cooking spray and heat to medium high. Add a tortilla to the pan. Spoon one-fourth of the veggies over half of the tortilla. Top with ¼ cup cheese. Fold the tortilla in half. Allow the folded tortilla to cook for 45-60 seconds per side (watch closely to avoid burning), until browned and the cheese is melted.

To serve, cut the quesadilla into thirds. Repeat the process with the remaining ingredients.

"When you do not seek or need external approval, you are at your most powerful." Caroline Myss

Black-Bean Quesadillas

Fresh veggies add a layer of lightness and excitement to this playful recipe, while earthy black beans, melted cheese, and toasty tortillas give it a warm, comforting feel.

Serves 2

3 tomatoes, diced
½ onion, diced
2 cloves garlic, minced
1 cup loosely packed chopped fresh cilantro, divided
Juice of 1 lime, divided
Salt and freshly ground black pepper
2 avocadoes, peeled and mashed

1 (8 oz.) can black beans, rinsed and drained
¾ cup shredded cheddar cheese
4 (8 inch) whole-wheat tortillas
Olive-oil cooking spray
Greek yogurt or sour cream for serving (optional)
Tortilla chips for serving (optional)

Prepare the homemade pico de gallo: combine the tomatoes, onion, garlic, ½ cup cilantro, juice of ½ lime, and salt and freshly ground black pepper to taste. Toss well. Set aside.

In a separate bowl, prepare the homemade guacamole: combine the mashed avocado, ½ cup cilantro, juice of ½ lime, salt and freshly ground black pepper to taste, and half of the pico de gallo. Toss well. Set aside.

To prepare the quesadillas: sprinkle a handful of beans and 2-3 tbsp. cheese over half of each tortilla. Coat a medium skillet with cooking spray and heat to medium high. Fold the tortillas in half, and 1 or 2 at a time, place them in the skillet. Cook for 45-60 seconds per side, until the cheese melts and the outside turns golden-brown and toasty. Turn the heat down if necessary to avoid burning. Continue with the remaining ingredients.

Afterward, open each quesadilla and spoon some pico de gallo and guacamole inside. Fold them again and reheat once more (30-60 seconds per side).

Cut the quesadillas into thirds. Serve with Greek yogurt or sour cream as desired. Any remaining guacamole and/or pico de gallo goes nicely with tortilla chips on the side.

"If you want to be sad, no one in the world can make you happy. But if you make up your mind to be happy, no one and nothing on earth can take that happiness from you."
Paramhansa Yogananda

Chicken-Pesto Flatbread

This plush pie begs to be savored slowly. Just like its rich colors, the flavors are intense and exquisite. For a little extra comfort, pair this pizza with a glass of full-bodied red wine. Bon appétit!

Serves 2-4

¾ lb. skinless boneless chicken breasts
¼ cup Italian salad dressing
1¼ cups spinach
3 tbsp. chopped fresh basil
6 tbsp. extra-virgin olive oil, divided
1 clove garlic, peeled

Salt
1 medium red onion, sliced
2 large (10-12 inch) whole-wheat pitas
2 tbsp. pine nuts
1 tbsp. dried rosemary
⅓ cup crumbled feta cheese

Preheat oven to 475 degrees.

Marinate the chicken in the Italian dressing for at least 30 minutes.

In the meantime, blend the spinach, basil, 3 tbsp. oil, garlic, and salt to taste in a small blender or food processor until smooth. Set aside.

In a skillet, heat 1 tbsp. olive oil over medium heat. Add the onions and cook, stirring frequently, for about 5 minutes. Add the chicken and cook for several minutes on each side, until cooked through. Slice the cooked chicken into small pieces.

To prepare the pizzas, evenly distribute the ingredients over the pitas. Start by spreading out the spinach mixture, then add the chicken, onions, pine nuts, dried rosemary, and feta.

Place the pitas directly on the middle oven rack. Bake for 6-8 minutes, until warm with crispy bottoms. Drizzle 1 tbsp. oil over each cooked pita.

"Real style is never right or wrong. It's a matter of being yourself on purpose." G. Bruce Boyer

Greek Chicken and Spinach Pie

This magnificent main dish is warm, nourishing, and protective. It has enough fat to give it flavor and a sense of rootedness and enough freshness to round that out. This is a wonderful winter meal that's also great for entertaining.

Serves 4

1½ cups chicken broth
1 lb. skinless boneless chicken breasts
2 tbsp. butter
2 green onions, chopped
2 tbsp. flour
¾ cup crumbled feta cheese
5 oz. baby spinach

1 tbsp. dried dill
1 tbsp. dried parsley
Salt and freshly ground black pepper
1 egg, beaten
1 pkg. filo dough*
Olive-oil cooking spray

Preheat oven to 350 degrees. Grease a 9x9 baking pan.

Pour the broth into a medium pot. Add the chicken and bring the mixture to a boil. Reduce the heat and simmer for about 20 minutes, until the chicken is cooked through. Reserve the broth and set the chicken aside.

Heat the butter in a small skillet over medium heat. Add the green onions and sauté for about 2 minutes. Stir in the flour until completely incorporated. Add the reserved broth to the skillet and bring the mixture to a light boil. Continue to stir and simmer for 3-4 minutes, until thick. Set aside.

In a large bowl, combine the feta, spinach, dill, parsley, and salt and freshly ground black pepper to taste. Shred or chop the cooled chicken and add it to the bowl, along with the broth mixture and beaten egg. Toss well.

Lay 1 sheet of filo into the pan, with the edges hanging over the sides. Spray it with cooking spray. Add 9 more sheets (half the package), spraying every 2-3 sheets with oil and laying them down in the opposite direction. Add the chicken mixture over the filo stack and then the remaining filo sheets (continuing to spray every few sheets with oil and laying them down in the opposite direction). Spray the top sheet and then use kitchen shears to carefully cut off some of the filo hanging over the pan.

Bake for 35-40 minutes, until golden brown. Cool for 30 minutes.

*Thaw the filo before getting started. When you are ready for it in the recipe, open the box, gently unroll the filo stack, and cover it with a damp cloth. It can be hard to work with, but it's fun too! (Don't worry about sheets that rip, as they will be covered up. Ideally, try to keep the top few layers intact, but if not, that's okay too.)

"I say, follow your bliss and don't be afraid, and doors will open where you didn't know they were going to be."
Joseph Campbell

Veggie-Roni Quiche

Packed with good stuff, this colorful quiche is deliciously satisfying. The luscious intermingling of veggies, meat, and cheese makes a comforting one-dish meal that tastes as awesome as it looks.

Serves 4

½ onion, diced
4 cloves garlic, minced
½ jalapeno, seeded and minced
1 small tomato, diced
½ red bell pepper, diced
½ small to medium zucchini, diced
½ cup chopped pepperoni (from a stick)

1 cup shredded cheddar cheese
4 eggs
1 cup flour
1½ tsp. baking powder
½ tsp. salt
1 tbsp. butter, softened
2 cups milk

Preheat oven to 400 degrees. Grease a 9x9 baking pan.

Place the vegetables, pepperoni, and cheddar cheese in the pan. Toss the ingredients together so they are well combined.

Place the eggs, flour, baking powder, salt, and butter in a large bowl, and then whisk in the milk.

Pour the egg mixture over the veggies. Bake for 40 minutes.

Allow the quiche to cool for 10 minutes.

"Because the chances you take, the people you meet, the people you love, and the faith that you have, that's what's going to define you." Denzel Washington

Lasagna Rollups with Kale

Fresh kale adds vibrancy to this hearty main dish. Once it's cooked, pretty pops of green are the only reminder that a superfood is inside.

Serves 2

8 oz. whole-wheat lasagna sheets

1½ cups ricotta

3 tbsp. grated Parmesan cheese, divided

1 egg

¾ cup finely chopped kale

Salt

1½ cups marinara

4-6 oz. fresh mozzarella, sliced

1 tbsp. chopped fresh parsley

Preheat oven to 400 degrees. Grease an 8x8 baking pan.

Prepare the lasagna noodles according to package directions.

While the lasagna sheets cook, place the ricotta, 1 tbsp. Parmesan, egg, kale, and salt to taste in a medium bowl. Stir to combine.

Lay a cooked lasagna sheet on a clean work surface. Line the noodle with the ricotta mixture, and then roll it up. Return any excess ricotta (that seeps out) to the bowl. Transfer the stuffed roll to the pan, and continue the process for the remaining lasagna sheets.

Distribute the marinara over the rolls, then add the mozzarella, remaining Parmesan, and parsley. Cover the pan with foil and bake for 30 minutes.

"Even if they can't come, a dinner invitation makes people feel loved. Expand your table." Chris Seay

Spaghetti Casserole

It doesn't get any more comforting than cheesy pasta. This easy, saucy bake is filling and relatively well rounded. The ricotta adds texture and a punch of protein, while the spinach lightens the hearty sauce.

Serves 8

8 oz. whole-wheat angel-hair pasta
2 tbsp. extra-virgin olive oil
1 (24 oz.) jar marinara
1 (14.5 oz.) can diced tomatoes, rinsed and drained
1 cup ricotta
1 cup diced onion
3 cloves garlic, minced
3 cups loosely packed spinach, chopped
1 tbsp. dried parsley
1 tsp. dried oregano
1½ cups shredded mozzarella

Preheat oven to 350 degrees. Grease a 9x13 baking pan.

Cook the pasta according to package directions. Drain it and stir in the olive oil.

In a large bowl, combine the marinara, drained diced tomatoes, ricotta, onion, garlic, spinach, and herbs. Stir well. Pour the tomato mixture over the pasta and toss to coat. Transfer to the baking pan. Top with mozzarella cheese.

Loosely cover the pan with foil and bake for 35 minutes. Uncover and cook for 5 minutes more.

Let the casserole stand for 20 minutes.

"Stuffed emotions will reappear." Georgie Holbrook

The Best Macaroni and Cheese

This is the quintessential comfort food! My grandmother's recipe has been a family favorite for years, and I share it here with you. "Grandmommy" insists on the Cabot brand of cheddar cheese, and I take her word for it. For best results, buy a block of the extra-sharp cheddar and freshly shred it yourself. This comforting side dish will light up your taste buds and make you feel right at home. At least it does for me.

Serves 8

1½ cups whole-wheat elbow pasta
3 tbsp. butter
3 tbsp. flour

½ tsp. salt
2 cups milk
2 cups shredded cheddar cheese

Preheat oven to 350 degrees.

Cook the pasta according to package directions.

In the meantime, in a medium pot, melt the butter over medium heat. Gently stir in the flour and salt. Once that's well combined, gradually add the milk, stirring almost constantly until thick, 8–10 minutes.

Remove the pot from the heat. Add the cheese and stir the mixture continuously until it is thoroughly combined.

Transfer the macaroni to a medium casserole dish. Pour the cheese mixture on top to cover. Bake for 45 minutes.

"Awareness is empowering." Rita Wilson

Pasta Puttanesca

This hearty dish merges salt and starch—a comforting combination that can also weigh you down. Enjoy a meal like this in moderation, and opt for high-quality ingredients.

Serves 4-6

6 cups chopped tomatoes (12-14 plum tomatoes)
12 oz. whole-wheat angel-hair pasta
½ cup extra-virgin olive oil (plus extra as desired)

6 cloves garlic, minced
2 tbsp. tomato paste
¼ cup capers, drained
40 pitted kalamata olives
½ tsp. cayenne pepper

Press the chopped tomatoes through a sieve. Use your hands to squeeze out as much liquid as possible.

Cook the pasta according to package directions.

Heat the oil in a large skillet over medium heat. Add the garlic and cook, stirring often, for about 2 minutes. Stir in the strained tomatoes. Cook, stirring frequently, for about 5 minutes.

Add the tomato paste, capers, olives, and cayenne pepper. Cook for 8–10 minutes, stirring occasionally. Toss with the pasta. Drizzle extra oil over each serving if desired.

"Sometimes to lose balance for love is part of living a balanced life." Ketut Liyer in *Eat Pray Love*

Garlicky Spaghetti

During World War II, the Russian government turned to garlic when antibiotics became scarce, hence its nickname of "Russian penicillin." It makes this recipe bold, flavorful, and aromatic, yet comforting too.

Serves 2

1 bulb garlic
8 oz. whole-wheat angel-hair pasta
¼ cup extra-virgin olive oil
1½ tsp. salt

Dash cayenne pepper
Freshly grated Parmesan cheese
Red pepper flakes

Preheat oven to 350 degrees.

Cut bottom/stem off garlic bulb. Separate cloves but leave unpeeled. Place half of the cloves on a sheet of aluminum foil. Bake for 20 minutes. Let the cloves cool, and then peel them.

Peel and mince the remaining raw garlic.

Prepare the spaghetti according to package directions. In the meantime, heat the oil in a skillet over medium heat. Add the minced garlic, salt, and cayenne and cook for about 2 minutes, stirring frequently. Stir in the roasted garlic and mash it well. Toss the pasta into the pan.

Top each serving with freshly grated Parmesan cheese and red pepper flakes to taste.

"The mistake is thinking that there can be an antidote to the uncertainty." David Levithan

Linguini and Clam Sauce

Cooling, salty clams nourish your softer side. Pair them with olive oil, garlic, and pasta, and settle in.

Serves 4

¼ cup extra-virgin olive oil
6 cloves garlic, thinly sliced
Salt
3 cans (6.5 oz.) clams in clam juice
1½ tbsp. butter
Dash cayenne pepper
1 tbsp. dried oregano
1 tbsp. parsley

¾ cup dry white wine
⅓ cup water
⅓ cup vegetable broth
1 lb. whole-wheat linguini or angel-hair pasta
1 tbsp. grated Parmesan cheese (plus extra for garnish)
Freshly ground black pepper

In a large pan or Dutch oven, heat the oil over medium heat. Add the garlic and salt to taste, and cook for 4–5 minutes, until soft.

Add the clams (with their juice), butter, cayenne, oregano, parsley, white wine, water, and broth. Simmer the mixture for about 20 minutes, stirring occasionally.

While the sauce is cooking, prepare the pasta according to package directions.

When the sauce is done, stir in 1 tbsp. Parmesan cheese.

Ladle the sauce over each serving of pasta. Top with Parmesan cheese and freshly ground black pepper to taste.

"Create the highest, grandest vision possible for your life, because you become what you believe." Oprah Winfrey

Creamy Butternut Ravioli

This radiant recipe will get you glowing from the inside out. Fresh squash improves energy flow, while its natural sugars offer comfort and calm. Ravioli can be dense and filling, so use red pepper flakes to add bite and encourage a slower savor.

Serves 4

1 butternut squash
1 1/2 lb. ravioli, variety of choice
1 tbsp. extra-virgin olive oil
2 cloves garlic, minced
Salt

1 cup vegetable broth
1/4 cup evaporated milk
Red pepper flakes
Parmesan cheese

Preheat oven to 350 degrees.

Cut squash in half lengthwise and scoop out the seeds. Lay the squash, cut-side down, in a 9x13 baking pan. Pour in 1/2 inch water. Bake for 1 hour and 45 minutes. Allow the squash to cool. Peel off and discard the skin and puree the flesh in a blender or food processor. You will need 1 cup puree in this recipe.

Prepare ravioli according to package directions.

In the meantime, heat the oil in a pot over medium heat. Add the garlic and a sprinkle of salt. Cook for 1-2 minutes, stirring often. Add 1 cup squash puree and vegetable broth. Cook for about 5 minutes. Stir in the evaporated milk and cook for 2-3 more minutes, until heated through.

Spoon the sauce over each serving of ravioli. Top with red pepper flakes, extra salt, and Parmesan cheese as desired.

"You face your greatest opposition when you're closest to your biggest miracle." Bishop T. D. Jakes

Sausage and Peppers

This colorful main course is a perfect mix of meat, veggies, and sauce. Bell peppers are one of the most nutritious foods you can eat. Here, they complement the sausage to make a well-rounded dish that is bright, hearty, and wholesome.

Serves 2-4

1 lb. uncooked turkey or chicken
   sausage
3 tbsp. extra-virgin olive oil
1 onion, diced
6 cloves garlic, minced
1 jalapeno pepper, seeded and minced

4 bell peppers, ideally different colors,
   cut into chunks
1 (14.5 oz.) can diced tomatoes
1 tsp. dried oregano
3 tbsp. tomato paste
Salt and freshly ground black pepper

Preheat oven to 350 degrees.

Gently remove the sausage from its casing and cut sausage into chunks. Lay them on a greased baking pan. Bake for 20 minutes.

In the meantime, heat the oil in a large pot over medium heat. Add the onion, garlic, and peppers and cook, stirring often, for 5-6 minutes.

Stir in the diced tomatoes, oregano, and tomato paste. Bring the mixture to a light boil. Then reduce the heat, cover, and simmer for 20 minutes. Remove from the heat, and add the sausage and salt and freshly ground black pepper to taste.

"Every loving thought is true. Everything else is an appeal for healing and help, regardless of the form it takes."
A Course in Miracles

Mom's Tomato Sauce

This classic home-style sauce is hearty yet fresh. It is perfect with pasta. Designed with a mother's touch, it will make you feel right at home.

Makes 12 cups

5 lb. tomatoes (10-15 tomatoes)
2-2½ lb. sweet or hot Italian sausage
2 tbsp. extra-virgin olive oil
2 cups diced onion
2 cloves garlic, pressed
2 tbsp. sugar

2 tbsp. salt
2 tbsp. chopped fresh basil
1 tsp. oregano
⅛ tsp. red pepper flakes
1 (6 oz.) can tomato paste
1 (28 oz.) can tomato puree

Bring a large pot of water to a boil and fill a large bowl with ice water. Put the tomatoes in the boiling water for about 45 seconds, until the skins begin to crack. Remove and place the tomatoes in the ice bath. Peel off the skins and discard the skins.

Puree the skinned tomatoes in a food processor. Set aside.

Cut the sausage into 2-3-inch chunks and submerge in a pot of water. Boil for 5 minutes, remove, and set aside.

Heat the olive oil in a large pot over medium heat. Add the onion and garlic and cook, stirring frequently, for about 5 minutes, without letting them brown.

Add the sugar, salt, basil, oregano, and red pepper flakes. Mix well.

Add all the tomatoes (fresh and canned). Bring the mixture to a boil. Then add the sausage. Reduce the heat, cover, and simmer for 2 hours, stirring occasionally.

Serve with your favorite pasta, and freeze the rest in batches.

"Put blinders on to those things that conspire to hold you back, especially the ones in your own head." Meryl Streep

Spinach and Basil Pesto

The intense taste of this lovely spread comes from 3 cloves of raw garlic and a fair amount of fat. It is a dense mixture of fresh and grounding ingredients. The net effect is a heaping cup of comfort that's great on pizzas, pastas, sandwiches, and more!

Makes about 1 cup

3 cups basil leaves
2 cups spinach
3 cloves garlic, peeled
½ cup grated Parmesan cheese

2 tbsp. pine nuts
¼ tsp. salt
7 tbsp. extra-virgin olive oil

Combine all the ingredients in a food processor and pulse until mostly smooth. Stir in more olive oil as necessary.

"There is nothing more rare, nor more beautiful, than a woman being unapologetically herself; comfortable in her perfect imperfection. To me, that is the true essence of beauty."
Dr. Steve Maraboli

Taco Enchiladas

This crowd-pleasing casserole has all the elements of comfort food—it's warm, meaty, cheesy, salty, and a bit spicy. Just mind your portions. It will fill you up!

Serves 4-6

1 lb. ground beef or turkey
1 pkg. taco seasoning
1 (16 oz.) can fat-free refried beans
9 (6 inch) corn tortillas
1 cup salsa (plus extra for serving)

2 cups shredded cheddar cheese
¼ cup sliced green olives
¼ cup jarred jalapeno slices (optional)
Chopped avocado
Greek yogurt or sour cream

Preheat oven to 350 degrees. Grease a 9x13 baking pan.

Cook the meat with the taco seasoning according to package directions. Spread the refried beans over the bottom of the baking pan.

To prepare the enchiladas, spoon about 2 tbsp. taco filling into a tortilla, and then roll it up and place it in the pan, seam side down. Repeat with the remaining tortillas (don't worry if they break; they will be covered up anyway!). Spread the salsa over the enchiladas. Top with cheese, olives, and jalapenos as desired.

Bake for 20-25 minutes, until the cheese is melted and slightly bubbly. Serve with extra salsa, avocado, and yogurt or sour cream.

"I believe you have to be willing to be misunderstood if you're going to innovate." Jeff Bezos

Tostados

Tostados are a fun meal, with a lot going on. The variety of fresh ingredients makes them light and uplifting, while the beans and meat add balance and bulk.

Serves 2-4

Pico de Gallo

1 pt. grape tomatoes, chopped
2 tbsp. chopped fresh cilantro
3 tbsp. diced onion
Juice of ½ lime
Salt to taste

Guacamole

2 avocados, peeled and mashed
2 tbsp. diced onion
3 tbsp. chopped fresh cilantro
Juice of ½ lime
Salt to taste

Tostados

1 (16 oz.) can fat-free refried beans
1 tbsp. extra-virgin olive oil
½ cup diced onion
1 lb. ground turkey
1 tbsp. cumin
1 tbsp. chili powder
Salt
6 tostados
1 cup shredded lettuce
1 cup shredded sharp cheddar cheese
½ cup sour cream or Greek yogurt

Preheat oven to 350 degrees.

Mix all the pico de gallo ingredients in a medium bowl. Similarly, mix all the guacamole ingredients in a separate bowl.

Gently heat the refried beans in a small pot, stirring occasionally.

Meanwhile, in a large skillet, heat the oil over medium heat. Add the onion and cook until soft, 3-4 minutes. Stir in the ground turkey. Brown the meat and cook it through. Add the cumin, chili powder, and salt to taste. Set aside.

Warm the tostados in the oven for 5 minutes.

To assemble, spread warmed refried beans evenly over top of each tostado. Top with the turkey mixture, and then lettuce, pico de gallo, guacamole, shredded cheddar, and sour cream or yogurt. Any extra pico and guacamole can go on the side.

"No matter what people tell you, words and ideas can change the world." Robin Williams

Jambalaya

This wonderful one-pot meal is settling and richly nutritious. The abundant mix of meat, grains, veggies, and spices makes it filling—a great dish for relaxing at home and also for entertaining!

Serves 6-8

1 tbsp. extra-virgin olive oil
1 onion, diced
6 cloves garlic, minced
10 oz. smoked chicken or turkey
  sausage, sliced
1 (14.5 oz.) can diced tomatoes
1 green bell pepper, diced
2 tbsp. paprika

1 tbsp. cumin
½ tsp. cayenne pepper
1 tsp. salt
1 cup uncooked brown basmati rice
3 cups vegetable broth
1 lb. large raw shrimp, peeled and
  deveined

In a large pot, heat the oil over medium heat. Add the onion and garlic and cook until soft, 3-4 minutes. Add the sausage, tomatoes, bell pepper, paprika, cumin, cayenne, and salt and continue to cook, stirring occasionally, for about 5 minutes.

Stir in the rice and broth. Bring the mixture to a boil. Then reduce the heat, cover, and simmer for 45 minutes.

When the rice is tender, add the peeled shrimp. Cook for 5-10 minutes more. Then turn off the heat and let the jambalaya stand (covered) for 1-2 hours so that it can thicken and the flavors meld.

"If you make an agreement with yourself to be impeccable with your word, just with that intention, the truth will manifest through you and clean all the emotional poison that exists within you." Don Miguel Ruiz

Peanut Butter-Banana Ice Cream

It's hard to believe that this creamy dessert is only bananas and peanut butter! Thanks to the potassium, each smooth and buttery scoop helps diminish stress and improve your state of mind. It is a truly sweet sensation.

Serves 1–2

2 bananas, peeled and frozen
3 tbsp. all-natural peanut butter

Place the ingredients in a food processor and blend until smooth and creamy. Serve immediately for a softer dessert, or transfer the mixture to a bowl and place in the freezer for 40 minutes to gently firm it up.

"You get your intuition back when you make space for it, when you stop the chattering of the rational mind. The rational mind doesn't nourish you. You assume that it gives you the truth, because the rational mind is the golden calf that this culture worships, but this is not true. Rationality squeezes out much that is rich and juicy and fascinating." Anne Lamott

feel **Treated**

Feel joy and a rush.

Mindfully savor rather than inhale, in order to avoid an energy crash.

Kids beg for them and dogs will jump through hoops for them—everyone loves a treat! They inspire joy and excitement but, by definition, are meant to be consumed in moderation.

These pleasure-promoting specialties require discretion for them to maintain their allure. Just like taking too much medicine, over-treating with food can make you sick. It can intoxicate your body, unsettle your mind, and dull your shine.

So mindfully savor these delectables as more than just fleeting treats. When you self-regulate, you can fully appreciate them and experience true balance and wellness.

Onion Rings

Homemade onion rings are less weighty than ones you can order in a restaurant, when you use quality oil and a low-calorie batter and give them a quick, light fry. Yet the result is every bit as delicious! For a little extra zing, dip them in spicy mustard.

Serves 2

1 onion	Salt
½ cup milk	Extra-light olive oil
½ cup plain yogurt	1 cup flour

Trim off the ends of the onion and peel off the papery skin. Slice the onion into rings that are about ½ inch thick.

In a large bowl, mix the milk, yogurt, and salt to taste. Toss the raw onion rings in the milk mixture and let stand for 15 minutes.

Heat about ½ inch oil in a medium skillet over medium heat.

Once the oil is hot, one at a time, coat the milky rings in flour, and then place them in the skillet. Cook for a few minutes, watching closely. Flip the rings once the sides start to turn golden brown. This will likely take a few batches (don't try to cook them all at once; I find that subsequent batches usually come out better). Add more oil to the pan as necessary.

Place the cooked onion rings on a paper towel to cool. Add a sprinkle of salt before serving.

"Success consists of going from failure to failure without loss of enthusiasm." Winston Churchill

Mexican Pizza

My dad's famous nachos, which we have always affectionately called "Mexican Pizza," are a perfect mixture of fresh ingredients, salty meat, and chips. The final product is a wonderful treat with redeeming nutritional value. It's a fun dinner and super snack!

Serves 6

1 lb. ground turkey
1 pkg. taco seasoning
1 tbsp. extra-virgin olive oil
1 green bell pepper, diced
1 bag tortilla chips
2 cups shredded cheddar cheese

3 tomatoes, diced
4 green onions, diced
Sour cream or Greek yogurt, avocado, sliced olives, sliced jalapenos, and/ or salsa for garnish

Brown the turkey in a large skillet. Add the seasoning and cook according to package directions.

In a separate small skillet, heat the oil over medium heat. Add the pepper and sauté for about 10 minutes, stirring frequently.

Distribute the chips among 3 large microwavable plates. Top each with cheese, taco meat, sautéed pepper, tomatoes, and green onions. Microwave each plate separately, for about 2 minutes, until the cheese is melted. Serve with garnishes as desired.

"We become what we think about." Earl Nightingale

Tomato-Pesto Pizza

Tangy goat cheese and potent pesto are a heavenly combination on this full-flavored pizza. The tomato adds some lightness and balance, but it's still an intensely tasty pie that's not for the faint of heart—or every day.

Serves 4

1 can refrigerated pizza crust
¾ cup Spinach and Basil Pesto (see index)
1 cup shredded mozzarella cheese

1 tomato, thinly sliced
5 oz. goat cheese
1 tbsp. extra-virgin olive oil

Precook the pizza crust according to package directions.

Evenly distribute the pesto over the crust. Top with mozzarella, tomato slices, and pieces of goat cheese. Drizzle oil over the top.

Bake according to package directions, generally 8-10 minutes.

"The grass is greener where you water it." Neil Barringham

Jalapeno and Kalamata Pizza

This hot and savory pizza bursts with flavor and pizazz. The jalapenos help slow you down and keep your appetite in check, while the olives make you feel full and present. Top that off with the other pizza fixings (such as a generous layer of cheese), and you've got yourself a saucy and sensational treat!

Serves 2

¾ cup pizza sauce
1 thin-crust whole-wheat pizza crust,
   such as Boboli

1¼ cups shredded mozzarella cheese
20 slices jarred jalapenos
20 pitted kalamata olives

Preheat oven to 450 degrees.

Spread the sauce over the crust, and then evenly distribute the cheese. Top with jalapeno slices and kalamata olives.

Bake for 8–10 minutes, directly on the oven rack.

"If you want to know what's going on with someone, pay attention to what they point out in you." Michelle Ruiz

Cheesy Roasted-Garlic Bread

Roasted garlic makes the soft loaf of French bread intensely aromatic, while the fresh tomatoes add lightness. This recipe is great for entertaining. Serve it fresh out of the oven.

Serves 8

1 bulb garlic	1 tbsp. parsley
2½ tbsp. extra-virgin olive oil, divided	1 baguette
8 tbsp. butter, softened	4 plum tomatoes, diced
2 tbsp. grated Parmesan cheese	1 cup shredded mozzarella cheese

Preheat oven to 400 degrees.

To roast the garlic, peel a few outer layers of papery skin from the bulb and trim the tips off the cloves. Place the bulb on a sheet of aluminum foil and pour 1 tbsp. oil on top. Wrap it up and roast for 40 minutes, until the middle clove is tender when pierced with a knife. Let the garlic cool. Reserve the flesh and discard the peels.

Combine the roasted garlic, softened butter, remaining oil, Parmesan, and parsley. Mash and mix the ingredients thoroughly.

Slice the baguette open lengthwise.

Spread the garlic mixture onto the open-faced bread. Top with diced tomatoes and mozzarella.

Broil for 3-5 minutes on an upper-middle oven rack, watching carefully to avoid burning.

"In every area, working with what you habitually reject is one of the best ways to facilitate growth and transformation."
Bernard Glassman and Rick Field

Creamy Caper Pasta

This luxurious pasta mixes wholesome freshness with creamy indulgence. Salty capers and sweet sundried tomatoes complement the rich gorgonzola sauce. It's not light, but it's good.

Serves 6

1 lb. whole-wheat spaghetti
1 tbsp. extra-virgin olive oil
½ onion, diced
2 cloves garlic, minced
1 (24 oz.) jar marinara sauce
1 cup vegetable broth
½ cup evaporated milk

1 (2¼ oz.) jar capers
¾ cup sundried tomatoes in oil, drained
¼ lb. gorgonzola
2½ oz. baby spinach
Freshly ground black pepper

Prepare the spaghetti according to package instructions, and drain.

In the meantime, heat the oil in a pot over medium heat. Add the onion and garlic and cook for 3-4 minutes, until slightly soft. Add the sauce and broth to the pot, and then slowly stir in the evaporated milk. Continue to cook the mixture over medium heat, stirring frequently, for 3-4 minutes.

Add the capers, sundried tomatoes, and gorgonzola. Cook for 5 more minutes, still stirring often. Add the spinach. Cook for another 4-5 minutes, stirring often, until the spinach is wilted and cheese is fully melted.

Return the drained pasta to its pot. Stir some of the sauce into the spaghetti. To serve, spoon the spaghetti into separate bowls and top generously with sauce. Add freshly ground black pepper to taste.

"If you never give yourself the opportunity to experience silence, this creates turbulence in your internal dialogue."
Deepak Chopra

Dad's Lemon-Caper Shrimp

This warm and nourishing recipe contains a lot of protein, which helps rebuild muscle. At the same time, the butter, capers, and breadcrumbs make this a treat. As a whole, it's a tasty dish that's great for a special occasion.

Serves 2

6 tbsp. butter
6 tbsp. extra-virgin olive oil, divided
4 cloves garlic, pressed
3 tbsp. capers, drained

3 tbsp. dried parsley
2 lemons, divided
1 lb. shrimp, peeled and deveined
⅓ cup Italian-style breadcrumbs

Heat the butter and 4 tbsp. oil over medium heat. Add the garlic, capers, parsley, and juice of 1 lemon. Stir well and then add the shrimp.

Allow the shrimp to cook on the first side for about 1 minute, and then flip.

Sprinkle the breadcrumbs over the mixture and allow the shrimp to cook for another minute, until just about cooked through.

Add the remaining 2 tbsp. oil. Stir the mixture around, distributing the breadcrumbs and making sure the shrimp are done, about 1 minute.

Serve with lemon wedges.

"The mind's first step to self-awareness must be through the body." George A. Sheehan

Peanut Butter Cookies

These easy cookies are terrifically textured. On top of that, they require just 3 ingredients and less than 20 minutes—delicious all the way around.

Makes 9–12 cookies

I cup all-natural peanut butter
⅓ cup sugar
I egg

Preheat oven to 325 degrees. Grease a baking sheet.

Thoroughly mix all the ingredients together. Use your hands to form small cookies with the dough, and then place them on the baking sheet. Using a fork, gently press each cookie twice, at right angles, to get a checkerboard effect.

Bake for 12 minutes, until golden brown.

"It is so important for us to get that we don't have to solve any of our problems. If we can soften our heart, give up some of our old ways of being, and reconnect to the truth, our problems will give us up." Baron Baptiste

Chocolate-Peanut Butter Crispies

Satisfy your sweet tooth without falling into a sugar coma. These creamy crispies contain just enough dark chocolate to give you an endorphin boost.

Makes 20 pieces

1 cup all-natural peanut butter
1 cup agave nectar
8 oz. brown rice-crisp cereal (about 6
    cups)
1 cup dark chocolate chips

In a small pot, heat the peanut butter and agave over medium heat. Stir until the mixture is warm and thinned out.

Place the cereal in a large bowl. Pour the peanut-butter mixture over the cereal. Using a rubber spatula, toss to coat the cereal. Spread into a 9x13 pan, and refrigerate for at least 30 minutes.

When the rice mixture is ready, melt the chocolate chips on the stove or in the microwave.

Using a rubber spatula, immediately spread the melted chocolate over the rice mixture, getting a thin layer of chocolate over the entire tray. Refrigerate for at least 1 hour before cutting into serving pieces.

"Use, do not abuse; neither abstinence nor excess ever renders man happy." Voltaire

Zucchini Brownies

Zucchini adds moisture and lightness to these fudgy brownies, and you won't even notice it's there! The extra water content and vitamin boost make this fabulous dessert less oppressive yet every bit as delicious as the traditional treat.

Makes 20 brownies

2 cups white whole-wheat flour
1 cup sugar
¼ tsp. salt
1½ tsp. baking soda
⅓ cup cocoa powder

½ cup canola oil
2 tsp. vanilla extract
2 eggs, beaten
2 cups unpeeled, grated zucchini
½ cup chocolate chips

Preheat oven to 350 degrees. Grease a 9x13 baking pan.

In a large bowl, gently stir together the flour, sugar, salt, soda, and cocoa powder.

Separately stir together the oil, vanilla, and eggs.

Slowly stir the wet ingredients into the dry mixture. Add the zucchini and chocolate chips and stir until just combined. Transfer batter to the pan. Bake for 20–25 minutes.

"You don't always need a plan. Sometimes you just need to breathe, trust, let go and see what happens." Mandy Hale

Black-Bean Brownies

Black beans replace flour in this terrific-tasting treat. A healthy helping of chocolate chips makes these brownies melt in your mouth, while the beans and hemp add power, without disturbing the flavor.

Makes 12-16

Cooking spray
1 (15 oz.) can black beans, rinsed and
    drained
2 eggs
3 tbsp. canola oil
¾ cup cocoa powder
⅛ tsp. salt

1 tsp. vanilla extract
¼ cup agave nectar
2 tbsp. stevia
2 tbsp. hemp seeds
1½ tsp. baking powder
1 tsp. baking soda
½ cup chocolate chips

Preheat oven to 350 degrees. Lightly coat a 9x9 baking pan with cooking spray.

Combine all the ingredients, except the chocolate chips, in a food processor. Blend for 2-3 minutes, until smooth and creamy. Remove the blade and stir in the chocolate chips.

Transfer the mixture to the baking pan. Bake for 20 minutes. Allow the brownies to cool in the pan.

"We all have the extraordinary coded within us,
waiting to be released." Jean Houston

Pumpkin Roll

This moist autumnal cake is fun, pretty, and sure to impress. The spices and pure pumpkin add vitality, while the cream-cheese frosting will make your sweet tooth smile.

Serves 8

Cake

¾ cup white whole-wheat flour
½ cup sugar
1 tsp. baking soda
1 tsp. cinnamon
½ tsp. ginger
½ tsp. nutmeg
¾ cup canned pumpkin puree
3 eggs, beaten

Frosting

½ cup confectioners' sugar
¾ tsp. vanilla extract
2 tbsp. butter, softened
6 oz. cream cheese, softened

Preheat oven to 375 degrees.

In a large bowl, mix the flour, sugar, soda, cinnamon, ginger, and nutmeg. Stir in the pumpkin puree and eggs.

Pour the mixture onto a parchment-paper-lined rimmed baking sheet.

Bake for 15 minutes, until the cake springs back lightly when it's touched.

Immediately transfer the cake to paper towels. Roll the cake up in the towels (from the short side) to form a log. Cool for 20 minutes.

To make the frosting: with an electric beater, combine the sugar, vanilla, butter, and cream cheese until smooth.

Gently unroll the cake. Spread the filling on top of the cake, to within 1 inch of the edges. Roll it up again and chill the cake in the refrigerator.

"In a simple way we could say the purpose of life is really to learn love and forgiveness . . . we're here to learn unconditional love and unconditional forgiveness in the schoolhouse of our relationships." Rev. Howard Caesar

Pumpkin Pie

This Thanksgiving staple doesn't have to be a sugar rush. The spicy version here, packed with fresh pumpkin, is only moderately sweet, but it still brings out the smiles. For a sweeter version, use ¾ cup sugar.

Serves 8

1 sugar pumpkin or 1 (15 oz.) can
   pumpkin puree
2 eggs, beaten
½ cup sugar
1 tsp. cinnamon
½ tsp. ginger
⅛ tsp. nutmeg

⅛ tsp. ground cloves
⅛ tsp. ground cardamom
¼ tsp. lemon zest
1 cup evaporated milk
1 (9 inch) unbaked deep-dish piecrust
Whipped cream for garnish

If you're using a real pumpkin: cut it in half crosswise (be careful; pumpkins are hard to cut!). Scrape out and discard the goopy inside. Cut out the stem, and then lay the pumpkin halves cut-side down on a foil-lined baking sheet. Bake at 350 degrees for about 1½ hours, until tender when pierced with a fork. Once the pumpkin is done, let it cool and then peel off the skin. Puree the flesh in a food processor until smooth.

To prepare the pie, preheat oven to 425 degrees.

In a large bowl, combine the pumpkin, eggs, sugar, spices, and lemon zest. Mix well. Slowly stir in the evaporated milk.

Pour the mixture into the piecrust. Bake for 15 minutes. Reduce the temperature to 350 degrees, and continue baking for 40–50 minutes, until a knife inserted near the center comes out clean.

Let cool for 2 hours, and then refrigerate. Serve with whipped cream!

"Ultimately what you do is secondary. But how you do it is primary." Eckhart Tolle

Apple Pie

It's all-American and a la mode. This pie is a "piece of cake" to prepare, and it's classically delicious. The warm apple-cinnamon scent makes you feel treated. To keep the doctor away, be mindful of your helpings.

Serves 8

6 medium apples, peeled, cored, and sliced
Juice of ½ lemon
¾ cup sugar
⅛ tsp. nutmeg
½ tsp. cinnamon

Pinch of salt
3 tbsp. cornstarch
1 pkg. refrigerated rolled piecrusts (2 crusts)
1 egg, beaten
Vanilla ice cream for garnish

Preheat oven to 375 degrees.

Place the apple slices in a large bowl. Stir in lemon juice, sugar, nutmeg, cinnamon, salt, and cornstarch. Mix well.

Lay 1 crust in a pie dish and lightly press it down. Pour in the apple mixture. Loosely add the top crust and pinch the edges to the bottom crust. You may need to use a knife to trim a bit of the overhang.

Cut 6, roughly 2-inch slits in the top crust, radiating out from the center. Brush top with beaten egg (you will not use all the egg).

Bake for 50-55 minutes.

Let the pie cool for at least 1 hour. Serve with vanilla ice cream.

"There are no extra pieces in the universe. Everyone is here because he or she has a place to fill, and every piece must fit itself into the big jigsaw puzzle." Deepak Chopra

Apple-Cinnamon Bread

Yogurt gives this soft, fall-like bread extra moisture and structure—it's an excellent ingredient in baking. Use organic apples for best results, and serve with a hot cup of herbal tea!

Serves 9

1 ½ cups white whole-wheat flour
1 tsp. baking soda
½ tsp. salt
2 tsp. cinnamon
½ tsp. allspice
¼ tsp. ground cloves
2 tbsp. ground flax
2 eggs
¼ cup extra-light olive oil
1 tsp. vanilla extract

¾ cup sugar
¼ cup plain regular yogurt
½ cup no-sugar-added applesauce*
2 apples, peeled, cored, and diced

Topping (Optional)

2 tbsp. oatmeal
2 tbsp. sugar
1 tsp. cinnamon

Preheat oven to 350 degrees. Grease a 9x5 loaf pan.

In a medium bowl, combine the flour, soda, salt, cinnamon, allspice, cloves, and flax. In a large bowl, whisk the eggs, oil, vanilla, and sugar.

Whisk the yogurt and applesauce into the egg mixture, and then gently stir in the dry ingredients. Fold in the apples. Transfer batter to the loaf pan.

Mix the topping ingredients if using, and sprinkle them over the batter. Bake for 45–50 minutes, until a knife inserted in the center comes out clean. Cool bread in the pan for 10 minutes, then carefully remove it and cool on a wire rack.

*If you don't have applesauce, slice and core an extra apple and boil it until soft. Run the cooked slices under cool water, remove the skins, and mash the slices. A large apple yields about ½ cup.

"Ruin is a gift. Ruin is the road to transformation."
Elizabeth Gilbert

Banana Bread

Bananas detox the body, are easy to digest, and are very naturally sweet—they are great for baking (and helping your body handle the baking). This moist and cakelike bread is not overly sweet. Add ¼ cup sugar or chocolate chips as desired.

Serves 8

2 cups white whole-wheat flour
2 tsp. baking powder
½ tsp. baking soda
½ tsp. salt
¾ cup sugar
2 eggs

⅓ cup extra-light olive oil
1 tsp. vanilla extract
4 very ripe medium bananas, mashed
  (about 1¼ cups)
½ cup nonfat Greek yogurt

Preheat oven to 350 degrees. Grease a 9x5 loaf pan.

Combine the flour, powder, soda, and salt in a medium bowl, and stir gently.

In a separate large bowl, whisk the sugar, eggs, oil, and vanilla. Stir in the mashed bananas and yogurt, and then stir in the flour mixture until just combined. Pour into the loaf pan.

Bake for 55–60 minutes.

Let the bread cool for 10 minutes in the pan. Then carefully remove it, and cool completely on a wire rack.

"Genius is eternal patience." Michelangelo

Banana Cream Pie

This bright and luscious golden pie is silky smooth. The crumbly graham-cracker crust is a perfect match for the creamy custard. For a sweeter version, use ½ cup sugar, but either way, enjoy this treat in moderation!

Serves 8

2 cups milk
¼ cup sugar
3 tbsp. cornstarch
¼ tsp. salt
2 egg yolks, beaten

2 tbsp. butter
1 tsp. vanilla extract
2 just-ripe bananas, sliced, divided
1 graham-cracker piecrust
Whipped cream for garnish

Combine the milk, sugar, cornstarch, and salt in a saucepan over medium-high heat and stir continuously until the mixture starts to thicken, 8-10 minutes.

Stir in the beaten egg yolks, and then add the butter and vanilla. Keep stirring for 2–3 more minutes.

Remove pudding from the heat and let it cool.

Spread half of the banana slices over the bottom of the piecrust. Add half of the pudding. Repeat. Refrigerate the pie for a few hours to let it set.

Top each serving with whipped cream as desired.

"I am not a product of my circumstances. I am a product of my decisions." Stephen R. Covey

Vanilla Pudding

Skip the preservatives and other junk—make pudding yourself! It's easy to do, and this recipe contains just enough sweetness to treat your taste buds.

Serves 4

¼ cup sugar
3 tbsp. cornstarch
½ tsp. salt

2½ cups milk
4 tsp. vanilla extract
2 egg yolks, beaten

Combine the sugar, cornstarch, and salt in a medium pot. Turn the heat to medium high and stir in the milk.

Add the vanilla and beaten egg yolks. Once the mixture is thoroughly combined, lower the heat to medium. Continue to cook, stirring almost continuously, for 8-10 minutes, until thick. Pour the mixture into 4 serving bowls and refrigerate for at least 2 hours.

"Happiness is when what you think, what you say, and what you do are in harmony." Mahatma Gandhi

Chocolate Pudding

This chocolate pudding has a light consistency and a subtle bittersweet bite. It has just enough sugar to serves as a treat and is perfectly portioned . . . when you just have one.

Serves 4

¼ cup cornstarch
¼ cup sugar
3 tbsp. unsweetened cocoa powder

1 square (1 oz.) dark chocolate (or 2-3 tbsp. chocolate chips)
2½ cups milk

Combine the cornstarch, sugar, cocoa powder, and dark chocolate in a pot. Turn the heat to medium high and slowly whisk in the milk, stirring continuously.

Bring the mixture to a light boil and stir constantly for 1–2 minutes, until thick.

Ladle the pudding into serving cups. Cool completely in the refrigerator.

"I don't even know if I'm talented, but I've told so many people I am, and they believe me." Mel Brooks

White Chocolate, Ricotta, and Berries

Melted white chocolate adds sweet smoothness to ricotta in this airy dessert that's awakened by fresh berries and a hint of buttery coconut. It's a fast and pretty dessert—a great last-minute treat for 2.

Serves 2

⅓ cup white-chocolate chips
1 tsp. coconut butter

1 cup ricotta
6 strawberries, sliced

In a small pot, combine the white chocolate and coconut butter. Cook the mixture over medium heat, stirring almost constantly until the chips are melted.

Pour the melted mixture into a medium bowl. Stir in the ricotta and then gently stir in the berries.

"The most common way people give up their power is by thinking they don't have any." Alice Walker

Blueberry Crisp

Cooked berries and a crumbly topping make this dessert a true delight. Blueberries are a legit feel-good food, and serving them up with a little extra sweetness can add spring to your step!

Serves 6-8

2 pt. blueberries
1 cup white whole-wheat flour
1 cup sugar
1 tsp. baking powder
¼ tsp. salt

1 egg
⅓ cup butter, melted
Un-melted butter as necessary
Vanilla ice cream for garnish

Preheat oven to 350 degrees.

Place the berries in a pie plate.

In a medium bowl, combine the flour, sugar, powder, and salt. Stir in the egg until the mixture is crumbly.

Cover the berries with the flour mixture. Pour the melted butter on top. If certain sections remain dry, dot those areas with extra (un-melted) butter.

Bake for 35–40 minutes, until golden brown and the berries are bubbly around the edges. Serve with vanilla ice cream.

"Anytime we show up for life with integrity and impeccability, doors open." Marianne Williamson

Peach Margaritas

Substitute fresh peaches for simple syrup in this delicious drink that will get you buzzing, in more ways than one.

Serves 2

2 peaches, peeled and cut into chunks
3 tbsp. tequila
4½ tsp. orange liqueur
5½ tsp. peach schnapps

4½ tsp. freshly squeezed lime juice
1 cup ice
Salt for garnish
2 lime slices for garnish

Place peaches, liquids, and ice in a blender, and pulse until smooth. Salt the rim of each glass by dipping it into a shallow bowl with water and then into salt that has been spread out on a dish or wax paper. Pour the mixture into the glasses, and garnish each with a slice of lime.

"Success is liking yourself, liking what you do, and liking how you do it." Maya Angelou

Classic Chocolate Milkshake

Here is an easy dessert that doesn't get the respect it deserves. The cold creaminess of a chocolate shake with a pop of vanilla is refreshing and decadent all at once. For best results, use premium chocolate ice cream and organic milk—it's creamier!

Serves 1

I cup high-quality chocolate ice cream
I cup organic low-fat milk
½ tsp. vanilla extract

Place the ingredients in a blender, and blend until smooth and creamy.

"Worrying is as effective as trying to solve an algebra equation
by chewing bubblegum." Laz Buhrmann

feel INDULGED

Feel supremely pampered.

Indulge with discretion, so as not to slide into a food coma.

To indulge is to experience unrestrained pleasure. Eating these luxuriant foods evokes exhilaration. But the threshold is low. Indulgences lose their luster and actually bring on dissatisfaction when overdone. Too many of these foods may expand your body, with layers of fat and self-loathing burying your vibrancy.

While enjoying these recipes, eat slowly and savor. Focus on the flavors, textures, and aromas, and mindfully appreciate every bite. Doing so will naturally balance that supremely pampered sensation.

Baked Puff-Pastry Brie

This Parisian appetizer can double as an indulgent main dish (girls' night?!). The flaky pastry and buttery brie make it intensely tasty and substantial. It's a luxuriant experience, French-style.

Serves 2-4

1 medium round brie	1 egg
1 sheet puff pastry	1 tbsp. water

Place the brie in the freezer for 5-10 minutes. In the meantime, preheat oven to 425 degrees.

Lay the pastry out on a cutting board and slice it in half lengthwise. Remove the brie from the freezer and slice it in half as well, so that you have 2 semicircles. Set each half of brie on 1 strip pastry and wrap pastry over brie, sealing pastry edges on the top of the brie.

Whip the egg with the water to make an egg wash. Coat the tops, sides, and bottoms of pastry with egg wash.

Place on a baking sheet lined with parchment paper and bake for 20-25 minutes, until golden brown.

"Cooking is the art of the family painted by the hand of love."
Kathryn Sandridge

Mozzarella Sticks

Gooey cheese and crispy batter make this fried indulgence addictive. Mozzarella sticks are great for parties or lazy afternoons, just not every day.

Serves 4

1 cup flour
2 eggs, beaten
1 cup seasoned panko breadcrumbs
1 pkg. mozzarella string cheese, each
   stick cut in half

Canola oil
Marinara sauce for serving

Place the flour, beaten eggs, and breadcrumbs in 3 separate small bowls.

One at a time, coat the mozzarella sticks in flour, dip them in the beaten eggs, and then roll them in the breadcrumbs.

In a medium skillet, heat about a quarter-inch of canola oil over medium heat. Add the coated mozzarella sticks to the pan one at a time (the oil should sizzle when you place them in). Once the edges start to brown, flip gently with tongs. Let the mozzarella cook for about 1 minute on the second side, and then carefully transfer the pieces to a dish that's topped with a paper towel.

Serve with marinara.

"Age is something that doesn't matter, unless you are a cheese."
Luis Bunuel

Spinach and Artichoke Dip

Superfoods meet buttery, gooey goodness in this appetizer that's awesome for entertaining. Serve it with pita chips, crackers, or toasted baguette slices and be ready for a sensational indulgence.

Serves 8–10

2 tbsp. butter
½ cup chopped green onions
2 cloves garlic, minced
1 (14 oz.) can artichoke hearts,
   roughly chopped
1 (10 oz.) pkg. frozen spinach,
   defrosted and squeezed dry
8 oz. reduced fat cream cheese,
   softened

Salt and freshly ground black pepper
¼ cup grated Parmesan cheese
½ cup grated Swiss cheese
½ cup shredded mozzarella cheese
Chips, crackers, or toasted baguette
   slices for serving

Preheat oven to 400 degrees.

Melt the butter in a skillet over medium-low heat. Add the green onions and cook for 5 minutes, and then add the garlic. Cook for 1 minute more.

In a large bowl, combine the green-onion mixture with the artichokes, spinach, cream cheese, salt and freshly ground black pepper to taste, Parmesan, and Swiss. Stir well. Pour the mixture into a medium casserole dish. Top with mozzarella.

Bake for 25 minutes. Broil for 1 final minute to lightly brown the top. Serve with chips, crackers, or toasted baguette slices.

"Most folks are as happy as they make up their minds to be."
Abraham Lincoln

Pepperoni Bread

This salty indulgence that's meaty, cheesy, and gorgeously grounding will make your mouth water. It's a great snack and also goes well with a salad for supper.

Serves 6

Handful of flour
Raw pizza dough
2 cups sliced pepperoni

¼ lb. deli ham
¼ lb. deli American cheese
2 cups shredded sharp cheddar cheese

Preheat oven to 350 degrees. Line a baking sheet with aluminum foil and grease it.

Sprinkle some flour onto a clean work surface. Using a rolling pin, spread the dough out over the flour. On top, evenly distribute the pepperoni, ham, and cheeses.

Use your hands to gently roll up the dough into a long loaf. Carefully transfer it to the baking sheet. Bake for 30 minutes or until golden brown.

"Secretly we're all a little more absurd than we make ourselves out to be." J. K. Rowling

Double-Chocolate Brownies

These gooey, fudgy, supremely decadent squares offer a jolt of joy and test you with temptation. Their buttery texture melts in your mouth. Practice savoring. A mindful serving brings an energetic rush, but too much causes a crash.

Serves 16

14 tbsp. butter, melted
½ cup unsweetened cocoa powder
1¼ cups sugar
3 eggs

2 tsp. vanilla extract
Pinch of salt
½ cup white whole-wheat flour
1 cup dark chocolate chips

Preheat oven to 350 degrees. Grease an 8x8 baking pan.

In a large bowl, combine the melted butter and cocoa. Whisk in the sugar. Set aside.

In a small bowl, lightly beat the eggs with the vanilla. Whisk this mixture into the cocoa mixture.

Stir in a pinch of salt, and then the flour and chocolate chips. Spread the batter into the baking pan. Bake for 30-35 minutes. Let the brownies cool in the pan on a wire rack.

"Acceptance means events can make it through you without resistance." Michael Singer

Chocolate-Ganache Brownies

Cocoa, coffee, Greek yogurt, semisweet chocolate, and half-and-half push this treat over the top. Its rich flavor and moist texture make it elegantly indulgent, and a little bit goes a long way. To bring out its bite, enjoy it with a bold coffee or full-bodied red wine!

Serves 12

1 cup white whole-wheat flour
1 tsp. baking soda
½ tsp. baking powder
½ tsp. salt
1 egg
¾ cup sugar
5-6 oz. plain nonfat Greek yogurt

¼ cup canola oil
1½ tsp. vanilla extract
½ cup brewed coffee, cooled
½ cup cocoa powder
12 oz. semisweet chocolate chips
¾ cup half-and-half

Preheat oven to 350 degrees. Grease an 8x8 baking pan.

In a medium bowl, gently combine the flour, soda, powder, and salt.

In a large bowl, combine the egg, sugar, yogurt, oil, and vanilla. Whisk in the coffee and cocoa, and then stir in the dry ingredients. Transfer batter to the baking pan. Bake for 20 minutes, until a toothpick inserted in the center comes out clean.

Let the brownies cool completely in the pan.

To make the ganache, combine the chocolate chips and half-and-half in a pot on the stove. Over medium heat, stir the mixture continuously, until the chocolate is melted and creamy.

Pour the chocolate sauce over the cooled brownies. Refrigerate until completely cool, at least 1 hour.

"I want to put a ding in the universe." Steve Jobs

Chocolate-Chip Toffee Blondies

Skip the boxed brownies and whip up these babies for a moist and chocolaty indulgence that will (temporarily) spike your energy.

Serves 16

1 cup white whole-wheat flour
½ tsp. baking powder
¼ tsp. baking soda
⅛ tsp. salt
5 tbsp. butter, melted
½ cup brown sugar

1 egg
1 tsp. vanilla extract
½ cup chocolate chips
1 toffee candy bar, crushed thoroughly
    with a mortar and pestle

Preheat oven to 350 degrees. Grease an 8x8 baking pan.

In a small bowl, gently combine the flour, powder, soda, and salt.

In a large bowl, stir together the butter, sugar, egg, and vanilla. Alternately stir in the flour mixture and chocolate chips in batches, until just combined.

Spread the mixture into the baking pan. Use your fingers to pat it down. Sprinkle the crushed toffee over the top. Bake for 10-12 minutes. Cool completely before cutting into squares.

"I have the simplest tastes. I am always satisfied with the best."
Oscar Wilde

Sweet-Potato Chocolate-Chip Squares

These succulent squares smell and taste like autumn. Warming spices make them perfect for a cool fall day.

Serves 15

2 cups white whole-wheat flour
2 tsp. cinnamon
¼ tsp. ginger
¼ tsp. nutmeg
⅛ tsp. allspice
I tsp. baking soda
¼ tsp. salt

I cup sugar
I cup butter, softened
I egg
2 tsp. vanilla extract
I (15.5 oz.) can sweet-potato puree
   (no sugar added)
12 oz. semisweet chocolate chips

Preheat oven to 350 degrees. Grease a 9x13 baking pan.

In a medium bowl, combine the flour, cinnamon, ginger, nutmeg, allspice, soda, and salt.

In a large bowl, beat the sugar and butter with an electric mixer. Beat in the egg, vanilla, and sweet-potato puree. Stir in the dry ingredients until just combined, then fold in the chocolate chips.

Transfer the batter to the baking pan. Bake for 30–35 minutes.

"Dessert is probably the most important stage of the meal, since it will be the last thing your guests remember before they pass out all over the table." William Powell

Chocolate, Peanut Butter, and Berry Fudge

This dense and intensely sweet recipe is the holiday season in a bite-size bar. The chocolate and peanut butter give it a velvety quality, while the cranberries brighten it up!

Serves 20

12 oz. semisweet chocolate chips
½ cup sweetened condensed milk
⅓ cup smooth all-natural peanut
 butter

¾ cup dried cranberries
2 tbsp. water

Place all the ingredients in a microwave-safe bowl. Microwave for 30 seconds, and then remove and stir. Heat for another 30 seconds, and stir again. Continue 1–2 more times if required to make the mixture smooth.

Transfer the fudge to an 8x8 baking pan and smooth it out. Refrigerate for at least 1 hour.

Note: You can alternatively prepare the fudge on the stove. Just be sure to stir continuously.

"Cherish your human connections—your relationships with friends and family." Barbara Bush

Chocolate-Peanut Butter Balls

There are few things in life more fantastic than peanut butter paired with chocolate. This recipe makes you work (the balls take some time to roll and coat), but it's worth it. So. Worth. It.

Makes 100

2 cups smooth peanut butter
¾ cup butter, divided
16 oz. confectioners' sugar

3 cups rice-crisp cereal
24 oz. semisweet chocolate chips
2+ tbsp. milk

Combine the peanut butter and ½ cup butter in a microwave-safe bowl. Microwave for about 1 minute, and then stir well.

In a large bowl, combine the sugar and cereal. Pour in the peanut-butter mixture and stir well.

Using your hands, form roughly 1-inch balls, and place them on a wax-paper-lined tray. Refrigerate for 1 hour.

In a microwave-safe bowl, combine the chocolate chips with the remaining ¼ cup butter and 2 tbsp. milk. Microwave for 30 seconds, and then stir. Continue 5-6 more times, adding milk as necessary if the mixture seems dry, until the chocolate is melted.

Dip the balls in the melted chocolate mixture and coat them completely. Place the balls on a clean baking sheet and refrigerate until cool and set.

"Burn brightly without burning out." Richard Biggs

Grandmommy's Kentucky Pie

This family-favorite dessert is easy and awesome. The bourbon gives it a little extra kick, while the pie filling is basically a giant gooey and nutty chocolate-chip cookie. Yum.

Serves 8

1 (9 inch) unbaked piecrust
2 eggs
¾ cup sugar
½ cup butter, melted
4 tbsp. bourbon, divided

¼ cup cornstarch
1 cup chopped walnuts
1 cup chocolate chips
8 oz. whipped topping

Preheat oven to 350 degrees. Place the piecrust in a 9-inch pie plate, if it didn't come that way already.

In a large bowl, whisk together the eggs, sugar, butter, and 2 tbsp. bourbon. Stir in the cornstarch, walnuts, and chocolate chips. Pour the mixture into the piecrust. Bake for 45-50 minutes.

Stir the remaining bourbon into the whipped topping. Once the pie has cooled, spread the spiked whipped topping on top.

"Have the courage to accept that you're not perfect, nothing is, and no one is—and that's okay." Katie Couric

Ice Cream Sandwich Cake

Perfect for summertime gatherings, this simple dessert is mouthwateringly cool and sweet. The final product looks and tastes so sensational, no one will realize that essentially all you did was stack a few ice cream sandwiches and crush some candy!

Serves 8–10

1 (12 pack) box ice cream sandwiches
1 container whipped topping, divided
2-3 toffee candy bars, crushed

In an 8x8 pan, lay down 1 layer of ice cream sandwiches. You will have to cut a few to fit the space. Layer half the whipped topping on top.

Add a second layer of ice cream sandwiches (you'll likely use 11 of the 12 sandwiches in the box).

Spread the remaining whipped topping on top. Sprinkle with crushed toffee. Cover and store in the freezer.

"Don't you dare, for one more second, surround yourself with people who are not aware of the greatness that you are."
Jo Blackwell-Preston

Carrot Cake

Sweet and slightly nutty carrots lend moisture, lightness, and a pretty orange hue to this beautiful cake. Cream-cheese frosting lifts it over the indulgent line. One slice is filling—and fabulous.

Serves 12

Cake

4 eggs
½ cup brown sugar
½ cup sugar
½ cup vegetable oil
½ cup plain regular yogurt
2 cups white whole-wheat flour
2 tsp. baking powder
½ tsp. baking soda

Pinch of salt
2 tsp. cinnamon
I tsp. nutmeg
2½ cups grated carrots

Frosting

I cup confectioners' sugar
8 oz. cream cheese, softened
½ cup butter, softened
2 tsp. vanilla extract

Preheat oven to 350 degrees. Grease 2 round cake pans.

In a medium bowl, whisk together the eggs, brown and white sugar, oil, and yogurt.

In a large bowl, stir together the flour through nutmeg. Stir in the wet mixture and grated carrots.

Divide the batter between the 2 cake pans. Bake for 18-20 minutes. Cool the cakes for 5 minutes in their pans, and then carefully transfer them onto wire racks. Cool completely.

To make the frosting: combine the sugar, cream cheese, and butter with an electric beater. Then add the vanilla, and beat for a few minutes until smooth and creamy.

After the cakes have cooled, cover the tops with frosting. Stack them and ice the sides as well.

"I am realistic—I expect miracles." Wayne Dyer

Chocolate-Chip Bread Pudding

Runny chocolate, smooth custard, and toasty brown sugar make this lavish dessert come alive. The blissful combination is endorphin boosting and divine!

Serves 6-8

2 cups lightly toasted baguette cubes
1¼ cups chocolate chips
3 eggs
¼ cup brown sugar, divided
2 tbsp. rum

1 cup half-and-half
1½ cups milk
Vanilla ice cream for garnish
   (optional)

Preheat oven to 325 degrees. Grease a medium (9x9) casserole dish.

Place the bread in the dish and sprinkle the chocolate chips on top.

In a separate bowl, combine the eggs, 3 tbsp. brown sugar, rum, half-and-half, and milk. Pour the mixture over the bread, and press the cubes down to submerge them in the liquid. Let stand for 20 minutes.

Sprinkle the remaining brown sugar over the top, and then bake for 40-50 minutes.

Allow the pudding to stand for at least 30 minutes after baking. Serve with ice cream as desired.

"All you need is love. But a little chocolate now and then doesn't hurt." Charles Schulz

Chocolate-Chip Cookies

These classic cookies go with milk and a smile. They are best fresh out of the oven—simple and sensational!

Serves about 15

1 cup + 2 tbsp. white whole-wheat flour
1 tsp. baking soda
¼ tsp. salt
1 egg

1 tsp. vanilla extract
½ cup butter, softened
¾ cup sugar
1 cup dark chocolate chips

Preheat oven to 325 degrees.

In a small bowl, combine the flour, soda, and salt.

In another small bowl, combine the egg and vanilla.

In a large bowl, use an electric beater to mix the butter with the sugar. Add the egg mixture and beat again. Stir in the flour mixture and chocolate chips (it helps to use your hands!). Drop by medium-sized spoonfuls onto an ungreased baking sheet. Bake for 14–18 minutes.

"Train your mind so that the time will come when instead of judging automatically, you will forgive automatically."
Gary Renard

Chocolate-Lover Cookies

This is a chocolate lover's heaven. This soft cocoa cookie is lusciously chewy, with lots of gooey chocolate chips. It is simple but extravagant.

Makes 45-50 cookies

2 cups white whole-wheat flour
⅔ cup cocoa powder
¾ tsp. baking soda
¼ tsp. salt
1 cup butter, softened

1¼ cups sugar
2 eggs
2 tsp. vanilla extract
2 cups dark chocolate chips

Preheat oven to 350 degrees.

In a medium bowl, combine the flour, cocoa, soda, and salt.

In a large bowl, beat the softened butter, sugar, eggs, and vanilla with an electric mixer. Gently stir in the flour mixture, then fold in the chocolate chips.

Drop by medium-sized spoonfuls onto ungreased baking sheets. Bake for 8-10 minutes.

"If one oversteps the bounds of moderation, the greatest pleasures cease to please." Epictetus

acknowledgments

Special thanks to recipe testers: Chelsea Sandridge, Vicki Fletcher, Ashleigh Spruell, Leslie Coleman, Jeanne Higgs, Chelsey Bunyer, Devon McAfee, Maggie Flecknoe, Kelly Seibert, Cheryl Hartnett, Paula Izard, Blair Izard, Laura Kirsche, Erica Kriscenski, and Tom Izard. For photography help, thank you to Candace Moore and Shauna Maness of Minerva House in Houston, Wladimir Moquete, John Gannon, and Kristin Hartnett. I would also like to acknowledge Nina Kooij, Steve Harris, Cinthia Moore, Michelle Ruiz, and my dear YogaOne community—I bow to you all.

Index